The Figure of Arthur

Also by Richard Barber

The Knight and Chivalry
(Longman)

Arthur of Albion
Henry Plantagenet
(The Boydell Press)

Samuel Pepys Esq
(Bell)

With Anne Riches:
Dictionary of Fabulous Beasts
(Macmillan)

The Figure of Arthur
Richard Barber

D. S. BREWER

Longman Group Limited
London
Associated companies, branches and representatives
throughout the world

First published 1972

ISBN 0 582 12583 9

Acknowledgements

The author and publishers are grateful to the University of Wales
Board of Celtic Studies and the University of Wales Press for per-
mission to reproduce extracts from *Rachel Bromwich: The Historical
Triads* (Bulletin of the Board of Celtic Studies XII) and to Professors
Gwyn and Thomas Jones for permission to reproduce extracts from
The Mabinogion.

Printed in Great Britain
by Ebenezer Baylis and Son Limited
The Trinity Press, Worcester, and London

Contents

... And as imagination bodies forth
The forms of things unknown, the poet's pen
Turns them to shapes, and gives to airy nothing
A local habitation and a name.

A MIDSUMMER NIGHT'S DREAM

Acknowledgements

I am most grateful to Dr Rachel Bromwich for reading the present book in manuscript, for making many helpful suggestions, and for providing new translations of the poems on pages 69–71 and 98–99. My debt is all the greater because the main thesis of this book does not coincide with her own much more deeply considered opinions as to the identity of Arthur. I hope that other readers will likewise accept it as a tentative contribution to the continuing – and probably insoluble – debate on the figure of Arthur in history.

RICHARD BARBER
January 1972

Chronological table

Square brackets indicate dates not accepted by the present writer

	EVENTS	PERSONS
400		
440	St Germanus visits Britain	
		Vortigern
		Ambrosius Aurelianus
[490	Battle of Badon]	[Arthur]
[516	Battle of Badon]	[Arthur]
[537	Battle of Camlann]	
547	Death of Maelgwn	
570	Death of Gildas	
574	Aedan accedes to throne of Dalriada	
590	Battle of Catraeth	Taliesin, Aneirin,
594	Battle of the Miathi	Arthur of Dalriada,
		Arthur of Dyfed
616	Battle of Chester	
		Artuir son of Bicoir
650	Conquest of Manau Gododdin	
655	Battle of Winwaed field	
664	Synod of Whitby; Anglo-Saxons all accept Roman usage for Easter	
700	*Life of St Columba* written by Adomnan	
768	Celtic church adopts Roman usage for Easter	
825	Merfyn Vrych comes to throne in Gwynedd	
829	Present version of *History of the Britons* written	

Literary developments

600 – Age of heroic poetry in Wales and North Britain; Irish annals; isolation from North Britain and Continent

700 – Early Welsh Easter Tables annals; genealogies; triads

800 – Beginnings of epic poems and sagas; antiquarian studies; History of the Britons compiled. Pseudo-heroic poems (Llywarch Hen); prophetic poems (*Armes Prydein*)
Links with Continent reopened

900 – Annals of Wales compiled; early saints' lives; *Laws of Hywel Dda*

1000 – Second antiquarian period; late saints' lives; early charter forgeries; Norman invasion

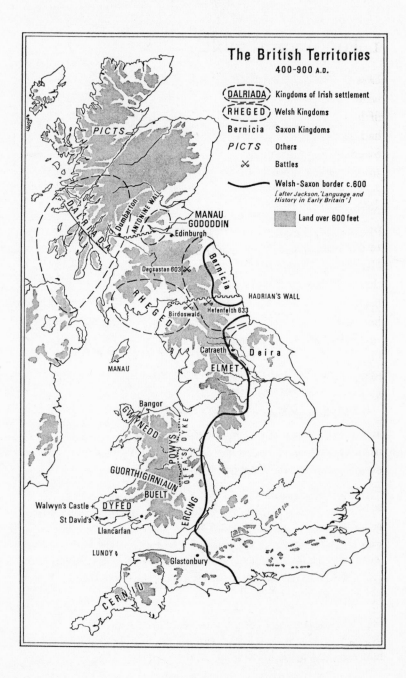

The British Territories
400-900 A.D.

(DALRIADA) Kingdoms of Irish settlement

(RHEGED) Welsh Kingdoms

Bernicia Saxon Kingdoms

PICTS Others

⤬ Battles

━━━ Welsh-Saxon border c.600
[after Jackson,'Language and History in Early Britain']

▨ Land over 600 feet

PICTS

DALRIADA

Dumbarton

ANTONINE WALL

MANAU GODODDIN

Edinburgh

RHEGED

Degsastan 603 ⤬

Bernicia

Birdoswald

Hefenfelth 633

HADRIAN'S WALL

Catraeth

Deira

MANAU

ELMET

Bangor

GWYNEDD

POWYS

OFFA'S DYKE

GUORTHIGIRNIAUN

BUELT

ERCING

Walwyn's Castle

DYFED

St David's

Llancarfan

LUNDY

Glastonbury

CERNIU

1 The Arthurian Controversy

Less than a hundred years ago, a patriotic Welsh writer could write enthusiastically and uncritically of Arthur as a late fifth-century successor to the Roman emperors, whose sway had extended from Scotland to Italy and from Ireland to Sweden; and he could still find a credulous audience. We may smile at this now; but is the 'historical Arthur' who has replaced this mythical figure any more firmly grounded in reality? It is a question that has often been asked, usually to provide exercise for a private theory that Arthur's battles as recorded in the early texts were all fought in Kent, Cornwall, Hampshire, the Midlands or Scotland, as the case may be; but the evidence on which the basic assumptions rely has usually been taken at face value. If we do take it at face value, Arthur becomes a survivor of Roman civilization fighting a desperate rearguard action against invading barbarians, an image both historically and emotionally attractive. It fills an awkward blank in British history; and it gives him a suitably heroic part to play.

In broad outline, this 'orthodox' view places Arthur's career around the end of the fifth century, immediately after a commander named Ambrosius Aurelianus, for whom there is early evidence. Arthur's achievement was to continue Ambrosius's military success to the point where, in a sustained campaign or series of campaigns, he checked the Saxon invasions with a great victory at Badon Hill, about the year 516. It was his victory there (for which there is also early evidence, but without Arthur's name as commander) that gained a breathing space of some forty years for the Britons throughout the whole island. He himself died in an internal conflict some twenty years after his triumph. The usual reason given for his success is that, being a descendant of the Roman *gens*, or family, Artorius, he had retained some knowledge of Roman military practice, and perhaps had organized a small mobile cavalry force. After his death, the history of the Britons was nothing but a succession of defeats, until only Wales itself was left to them; he therefore stood out in their memory as the last great warrior of their race.

Yet this attractive theory is by no means so solidly based as its champions would have us believe. There are difficulties and problems which have to be waved aside. Firstly, there is an increasing awareness that it is not simply a question of piecing together the evidence, slender as it is, from Welsh and Latin sources, but of trying to discover where that evidence came from, what kind of authority it has, who wrote it down and why, and what kind of attitudes the writer might have held. Even the most apparently factual evidence is not always what it seems; a date in a set of annals can be affected by all kinds of accidents in the course of compilation or even of copying. Unless it appears in a manuscript written within a few years of the event described, it must be analysed in the same way as other evidence.

There are, too, certain general points which are all too often forgotten. Early historical records – early, that is, in relation to the development of a particular society – are usually religious in origin, deriving from calendars used to date religious festivals. Early historical writing is almost always preceded by a stage in which important contemporary figures are the subject of literary compositions. Homer comes before Herodotus, the tables for reckoning Easter before the annals of the monasteries.

Again, where historical records are sparse, literature can only help us to a certain degree: poets may describe for us the society in which they live, but they will never give a dry outline of how it was organized, the faults and virtues of its rulers, and above all they will rarely offend their patrons' vanity. So we may find ourselves balancing one set of approximate values, the poetic image of a period, against another set, the attitudes we would expect to find given that we have read the message of the poetry correctly. And we must also remember not to assume attitudes which are too modern or which belong to an earlier or different milieu. Historical truth as a kind of philosophic absolute only begins to appear in the twelfth century. Earlier writers used history – as they themselves would have freely admitted – to illustrate a point, as a weapon in a wider argument. This argument was often nationalistic, or religious, or both, as we shall see. An extreme example (though not one which gained very wide acceptance) is the continuous rewriting of the history of Glastonbury, beginning with tentative stories in the eleventh century about its associations with a wide range of Celtic saints, and progressing through its claims to connections with Arthur and to the founding of the Old Church by St Patrick to contacts with the apostles and Joseph of Arimathea and the fantasy of Christ's visit to Britain with the traders in Cornish tin:

> And did those feet in ancient time
> Walk upon England's mountains green?

Speculation and accepted history are remorselessly inter-mingled, either deliberately or by popular belief, each new element attracting more detail and widening the scope of the legend like ripples in a pool. From the small original pebble of the desire of Glastonbury's monks to confirm ancient rights to certain lands, the rings ran outwards through politics and religion to folk-tales and literature.

By working backwards from the last and most unlikely of the Glastonbury legends, we can piece together the gradual accumulation of stories and details, from popular stories to convincing rewriting of the first chronicler of the abbey, William of Malmesbury. But unless we can also provide motives, the whole analysis must stand open to question. As medieval society became more stable and dependent on records, the monasteries were faced by the difficulty of proving their claims to land and rights. With no means of enforcing them (unless their abbot happened to be politically well connected or even warlike) they were among the first to rely on royal justice, and the courts increasingly required written precedents. If their case was weak, on the other hand, the courts would prefer old parchments to the hearsay evidence which was usually all that their opponents could offer. So, irrespective of the justice of the claim, there were strong incentives to provide the necessary materials, perhaps using monastery traditions and stories as the basis.

We can sometimes test this evidence against more accurate records, and Domesday provides a useful check on the ownership of lands. But for the most part, a mixture of instinct (has the story an obvious purpose?) and detailed textual analysis (are there anachronisms in the style of a charter?) has to be used. Sometimes the intention aforethought is crystal clear, or the text uses the formulas of four centuries later; but on other occasions the balance of probability is much more even. For instance, stories about Arthur carrying the image of the Virgin could be a ninth-century invention; but there is also the possibility that the story is a genuine tradition. So we have to trace the relative attitudes to the worship of the Virgin in Wales in the ninth century and Britain in general in the sixth century. On the one hand, Mariolatry is comparatively rare in Wales until the twelfth century, and references to the Virgin herself almost unknown in literature; on the other hand, a particular devotion to her would have been extraordinary anywhere in Europe three hundred years earlier, except in Byzantium and its territories. Could the ninth-century writer have had good reason to insert this detail? Or might Arthur have been to Byzantium?

Because we lack a secure historical framework for the fifth and sixth centuries, the usefulness of auxiliary evidence such as archaeology and philology is severely curtailed. Archaeology rarely supplements historical detail; it provides instead the broad underlying trends, the forest which the historian cannot see for trees. But it is the individual trees that allow us to plot the boundaries of the forest. As the Roman influence recedes, and with it the items which can be related to a continuous series of chronological records, we are left with evidence for a series of developments which can be placed in rough order of succession on any given site, and which can provide broad outlines of invasions or of successful defensive campaigns, but which can never provide a *historical* picture as opposed to a cultural one. Furthermore, the remains of Dark Age Britain are much slighter than those left behind by the Roman engineers, and stylistic problems are much greater. We cannot always tell a Saxon earthwork from a Celtic one, while Roman masonry and military works have their own particular style. Increasing interest in the period and wider excavation of its sites will undoubtedly fill many gaps in our knowledge; but the difficulties of comparison and correlation mean that archaeological evidence can only be used with the greatest caution by the historian.

There have been suggestions that recent excavations, particularly at Cadbury Castle, can be compared with Schliemann's discovery of Troy in the last century. If there is a parallel, it is a very tenuous one indeed. The Homeric poems are detailed epics, offering a vast amount of precise information; and even if only part of this information is accurate, the sheer volume of it is vastly greater than anything we have on Arthur. There is only one striking event connected with Arthur in the early evidence, the battle or siege of Badon Hill, and recent scholarship has put even this in doubt. The site of Badon remains elusive. Camelot, with which Cadbury Castle has been associated, is a twelfth-century invention without any basis in native poetic tradition. We shall return to this theme; but there can be no question of any discoveries on a Trojan scale in early British archaeology.

Arthurian topography, too, is a subject which offers little or no substantial evidence as to the identity of the historical Arthur. Firstly, the Celts were intrigued by place names, and frequently invented stories to explain them involving some heroic deed; and after the ninth century Arthur was often chosen as the protagonist of such tales. Secondly, there is a more general pattern, in both legends and traditional names, by which early heroes whose exploits have been forgotten, are replaced by newly prominent figures; and to the medieval mind the latter often meant Arthur. So there are no photographs of obscure hilltops or wooded valleys in this book; our concern is with history, not folklore.

More difficult is the use of philology for the analysis of the names associated with Arthur in the earliest records. Obviously, any name which can be positively identified is a most valuable indication; but this does not justify ingenious torturings according to barely scientific rules to make an obscure word fit a modern identification. Furthermore, only an expert deeply versed in early linguistics can even begin to offer such interpretations. In the words of Professor Kenneth Jackson, probably the leading worker in this field, after an exhaustive attempt to identify the sites of Arthur's twelve battles as given in Nennius's *History of the Britons*, 'only two can be regarded as fairly certainly identifiable . . . The rest are all conjectural or unknown . . .' And even these two identifications do not depend on philological analysis, but on the evidence of other texts.

So we are left to rely for the most part on the analysis of the texts themselves; and this brings us back to our earlier point, that literary activity is usually found before historical records begin. This is of cardinal importance for what follows. The reader who already knows something of the early material on Arthur may be surprised to find himself plunged into sixth-century poetry instead of the more familiar, apparently historical texts, while the newcomer may find it even more baffling. But to present the later texts first is to distort the whole picture. On the other hand, it is only recently that the antiquity of some of the Welsh literary material has been realized; but from the patient work of a number of scholars it is now possible to reconstruct a truer perspective. We shall see that the classic Arthurian source, Nennius's *History of the Britons*, though it may appear a crude and even naïvely honest work, is motivated by certain political considerations; but above all it depends not on historical but on literary sources. It is nearer to the acknowledged literary efforts of Geoffrey of Monmouth than to the relatively sober histories of Irish or Anglo-Saxon monks.

Even when it comes to literary evidence, we are dealing with fragments; no one is ever likely to know the full extent of the Welsh stories about Arthur, particularly as the early heroic poetry was already itself fragmentary by the ninth century, while ninth-century remains were almost as sparse three centuries later. The same applies to a much lesser extent to historical records. So what follows is by no means a final answer, but only an alternative solution to the puzzle. However, the orthodox view of Arthur is in danger of becoming accepted as fact by default of a challenger; and if the present study only serves to raise again a few of the doubts which have been brushed aside by the champions of Camelot, it will have served its purpose.

For there is yet another trap for the unwary, this time a psychological one. Much of the enchantment of Arthur as hero has stemmed from his ability to shift his shape in accordance with the mood of the age. This is a most important feature, clearly discernible from the twelfth century to the twentieth, from Geoffrey of Monmouth to Malory, and from Tennyson to T. H. White. His latest shape is arguably moulded by this same kind of wish-fulfilment. There is a blank in British history in the early sixth century; and history abhors a vacuum. So a plausible lay figure has been created to fill it, a last heroic bearer

2

of the flame of Roman civilization against the black barbarian night. The details have been tricked out with whatever lay to hand – for instance, a wide-ranging list of possible battle sites became evidence for mobility and thus for a Celtic cavalry corps. Instead of subscribing to this attractive contemporary hero, I would suggest that even in the early texts this process of shape-shifting has taken place. The ninth-century Arthur is equally a topical hero for the times, a figure to fire the imagination of the writer's contemporaries.

Arthur is not alone in this strange mutation from obscurity to legendary renown. Roland offers a parallel case which may shed some light on the mechanisms of medieval myth-making. The historical Roland is quite unknown apart from a single reference to his death in Eginhardt's *Life of Charlemagne* (*c.* 830), where he is listed third among those slain in the retreat from Spain in 777: 'In this battle died Eggehard, who was in charge of the King's table, Anshelm, the Count of the Palace, and Roland, Lord of the Breton Marches, along with a great number of others.' The occasion of his death is described by Eginhardt in some detail; yet he cuts no heroic figure. In the *Chanson de Roland*, two centuries later, he has become the central character, nephew of Charlemagne. Some critics have seen this elevation of Roland as a Christian hero against the pagan enemy as the result of the First Crusade in 1099; but it would be fairer to look at the poem as part of the increasing hardening of attitudes between Christianity and heathendom from which the First Crusade arose. There is an undoubted basis of religious ideology in the legend of Roland, just as a nationalist ideology permeates Arthurian legend in its earlier phases. Equally, the legend of Roland became international and increasingly fantastic as the medieval writers developed it, until its strange last form in Ariosto's *Orlando Furioso*.

Other examples of purely literary development from a very small beginning can be found within the Arthurian romances themselves. Both Lancelot and Perceval, for example, start from the most obscure beginnings – mere names in lists of knights – to become the foremost heroes of the Round Table. What the poets who wrote about them were drawing on we cannot say, though there is evidently traditional material about them which has not come down to us. In the case of Galahad, who is the hero of the later versions of the quest for the Grail, even this background is missing, and his history is pure literary invention, probably under the influence of the Cistercian monks.

These analogies may help to explain why Arthur himself, originally remembered at best as victor of one major battle, came to dominate Welsh legend. If we accept that his name was first recorded in literature, and only later in history, the processes of literary imagination, better adapted to the creation of new heroes, would explain his almost meteoric rise. Characters with a clear place in historical record could not so easily be transposed from legend into history, as even a ninth-century historian was likely to prefer historical records to oral or written tradition.

Another thread in the obscure tapestry of early tales about Arthur is that of mythology. Discredited by the excessive claims of nineteenth- and early twentieth-century writers, this has been largely ignored in recent years except by scholars. Max Müller (whose methods for demonstrating the ubiquitous nature of solar myth were finally turned against him with all too effective irony when he himself was shown, on his own criteria, to be a solar myth as well) represented an extreme view; and even as recently as 1945 a distinguished scholar could argue that Arthur was a raven-god, citing in support the sober remark that 'as early as 1909 Dr Julius Pokorny believed he could see an anthropomorphized cuckoo behind Cuchulainn [the Irish hero]'!

But mythology in a degenerate form is easily transmuted into folklore and heroic tales, perhaps even the same type of heroic story which lay at its root. There is clear evidence for the presence of pagan deities in some Welsh tales, where they appear as heroes with strange attributes, and it was this that set off the search for Arthur as god. However, his supernatural functions are very few and far between, and it is much more likely that he has 'usurped' the characteristics of older, forgotten heroes, just as Galahad supplanted Perceval in the Grail quest and Lancelot supplanted Gawain as foremost knight of the Round Table. Such changes are easy to trace in written literature; but in the recited Welsh poems, even with the elaborate training in memorization of the poets, there is both the possibility of mistakes in the handing down of stories and the impossibility of recovering the lost original.

For this is the fascination of the figure of Arthur. Short of some fantastic invention, a time machine, say, or an equally fantastic discovery, an inscription naming him from a period which has left barely a word engraved on stone, Arthur himself will always elude us; we can sketch his shadow, or what seems to be his shadow. If at the end of the fine-meshed sifting of the evidence which follows, it seems that all that has been achieved is to offer a different but equally insubstantial shadow, this preface may have given some idea of the reasons why we can expect no more.

2 Arthur of Dalriada

In the last years of the sixth century a small force of British troops rode southwards through Northumberland and Yorkshire to attack the 'men of Lloegr', the English invaders who had been steadily advancing northwards in the previous decades. They were from the household of Mynyddog, a chieftain who ruled from Edinburgh over lands around the head of the Firth of Forth and south through Lothian. This territory, known as Manau Gododdin, was now in the forefront of the resistance to the inexorable conquests of the English of Bernicia and Deira, and many such raids must have been mounted during the bitter years of retreat from the richer lands of the south. This particular expedition was to achieve a wider fame, however, for with the troops there rode Aneirin, a poet famous among the Men of the North. His presence might well be interpreted as a measure of the Britons' hopes of victory, for the expedition had been in preparation for a year, as men gathered to taste Mynyddog's hospitality, and three hundred men with accompanying footsoldiers, few enough by Roman standards, was probably as many as the North British could muster: a mixture of mounted troops and infantry, they were lightly but adequately armed.

At Catterick (Catraeth), perhaps seventy miles into English territory, the raiders found the enemy army. How large it was we do not know, though the odds were probably against the Britons. They fought; and all save a handful of the British perished. Aneirin escaped, to write *The Gododdin*, a dazzling, bitter poem about the army that had vanished, mourning the heroes in a set of elegies whose recurring refrain was the contrast between the rich hospitality of Mynyddog's court and the bitter price the warriors had paid for it: 'the pale mead was their feast, and it was their poison.'[1] We learn little about actual events at Catterick, little about the men themselves, even though each verse is a specific or general commemoration of the warriors. We learn much about their society and its values. Individual prowess and fame is the chief virtue of this warlike, aristocratic world, where Christianity is little more than a veneer. There is no emphasis on discipline or restraint; indeed, a reckless ferocity is the warrior's highest quality. We are in the heroic age, all inheritance of Roman organization and civilization forgotten, and the poet plies his epithets as colourfully as the hero his bloody sword.

Much of the poem remains difficult; even the greatest Welsh scholars are baffled at this distance of time by precise meanings of words which, written down at an unknown period after Aneirin's death, only survive in one thirteenth-century manuscript.* We know very little about the men named, save for a handful of figures who reappear in later legend; and even more mysterious are the two or three names which are used as yardsticks of courage, of valour. In several cases Aneirin compares one hero with another who is also named in the poem as fighting at Catraeth; but two figures do not reappear. Of Eithinyn, Aneirin says that 'his courage was enchanted, like Elffin', and of Gwawrddur, 'he glutted black ravens on the rampart of the stronghold, though he was not Arthur'. An Elffin appears in later legend as Taliesin's master; and Aneirin knows of Taliesin as a famous bard, 'master of word-craft'. Taliesin is generally believed to have been a near-contemporary of Aneirin's, perhaps working in the kingdom of Rheged, centred on Carlisle. If this is correct, we could perhaps identify the Elffin of the poem with this almost contemporary figure though the name (from the Latin Alpinus) occurs elsewhere in early records. It would therefore seem reasonable to assume that Arthur, too, belongs to the same period, as there are no

---

* The earliest *surviving* examples of written Welsh date from the ninth century, but this does not mean that *The Gododdin* could not have been written down before then.

other references to earlier heroic figures. All the comparisons are immediate, to figures whom the poet's audience would have known personally. *The Gododdin* belongs to the formative years of heroic myth, when traditions are being shaped. There is no store of legend from which to draw comparisons: in later poetry, the references are backwards in time to these early figures, but here there is no clearcut evidence of such a process of glorifying warriors by comparison with their predecessors.

How far is this reading of the poem borne out by other surviving poems and evidence? The earliest mention of the British poets in the period after the Roman occupation is in Gildas's famous lament over the woes and wicked ways of his nation, *De Excidio Britanniae*, (*On The Ruin of Britain*), written about the middle of the sixth century, perhaps fifty years before *The Gododdin*. He says of Maglocunus (Maelgwn):

When the attention of thy ears has been caught, it is not the praises of God . . . that are heard, but thine own praises (which are nothing); the voice of the rascally crew yelling forth, like Bacchanalian revellers, full of lies and foaming phlegm, so as to besmear everyone near them.[2]

Not a very flattering or even a very informative reference: but Gildas had his own prejudices and purposes, being a new Jeremiah rather than a historian. All that can be gleaned is that the songs which Maelgwn found so sweet were eulogies of himself, and this fits well with the surviving poems. Behind these early works we can dimly discern an earlier tradition of uncertain nature, perhaps chiefly religious. The word *bards* – *bardoi* – first appears in the first century BC, used by the Greek writer Posidonius; and other classical writers speak of poets and seers associated with the priestly druids. There is however a clear distinction between these 'inspired' religious functionaries and the more practical court poets with a definite social function, paralleled by that of the English *scops* in the halls of their enemies. Until the late fifth and early sixth century the structure of society was still sub-Roman, and the courts essential to poets like Aneirin had not yet developed sufficiently to have their own distinctive culture. Any surviving pagan poets had little religious encouragement and none of the early court poetry bears traces of their influence. Such traces of pagan myth as reappear in later poetry may have derived from folk-literature based on the druids' traditions; but a direct and continuous tradition in terms of style and presentation from pre-Roman days to the immediate post-Roman period is not borne out by the evidence of either *The Gododdin* or of Taliesin's poems, which are similarly immediate, eulogies or elegies for his contemporaries.* There are rich epithets, but no appeals to tradition or to heroes of days gone by: nor are there any nostalgic references to the glories of Roman Britain, in sharp contrast to Gildas's perpetual harping on the lost paradise of Roman rule.

The next historical reference to the bards, in Nennius's early ninth-century compilation, *History of the Britons*, is one of the scraps of tradition which abound in that muddled book: and it preserved names which may be those of the first generation of important court poets. After an entry referring to Ida of Northumbria (reigned ?547–59), Nennius says: 'Then Dutigirn fought bravely against the English people. Then Talhaern Tat Aguen won fame in poetry; and Neirin and Taliesin and Bluchbard and Cian who is called Gueinth Guant, all at the same time won fame in British poetry.'[3]

Of these names, Taliesin and Aneirin we have already met; none of the works of Cian, Bluchbard and Talhaearn has sur-

* This is not to deny a continuity of poetic lore and attitude. As Professor Jackson says (*Gododdin*, p. 88) '... it is clear that there can have been no unbridged gap in the history of Celtic poetry in Britain, since it carries on the Celtic traditions shared with Ireland: and it would be strange if there were. The poets must have continued to compose, but now in the *dolce stil nuovo*, and it is not for nothing that Taliessin and Aneirin and their contemporaries were called the *Cynfeirdd*, the "first" or "earliest" poets (of the new Welsh and Cumbric language).'

vived. But all of them were revered in later poetic tradition as the *Cynfeirdd*, or 'early poets': and this reverence for the past, which developed as early as the ninth century, permeates Welsh poetry in such a way that it seems difficult to envisage a time when the poets of the Britons had no traditional forms to which to hark back.

If the early poets betray a state of mind not unlike that of their English counterparts, there is no fellow-feeling for the enemy. Throughout *The Gododdin*, Aneirin rejoices at men such as Tudfwlch Hir who 'slew Saxons at least once a week'; and Taliesin, in a dazzling image from his 'Lament for Owain ab Urien' exults the dead Saxons:

> The hosts of broad England
> Sleep with the light in their eyes

This implacable hatred for the enemy is the obverse of the coin of loyalty. It is part of the stock-in-trade of the poetry of the 'Heroic Age', a stage which Anglo-Saxon civilization soon outgrew; but the Welsh, as they were driven back into their hills and valleys, retained the feelings and structure of a primitive society grouped in small units for much longer than the more mobile Saxons and Danes.

Even so, to regard the Saxons as the only enemy, and the Welsh as an entirely isolated people is far from the whole picture. Behind this great confrontation of two peoples and traditions, there is a continual movement of lesser shifts in the centres of power and culture. At the beginning of the seventh century, there were British kingdoms in a continuous belt from Edinburgh to Penzance: Gododdin in east Scotland, Strathclyde in the west, Rheged on the border and down to Lancashire; the Welsh kingdoms; and the kingdoms of Devon and Cornwall. Beyond these, in Pembroke and in Argyll (Dalriada), the ruling dynasties had crossed from Ireland, probably during the late fourth and early fifth centuries. In the far north, the

Picts were divided into tribes who occasionally united to raid the richer lands of the British. And the richest land of all, in the south and east, lay in Saxon hands.

The shifting alliances and feuds of the numerous kings and kinglets who ruled the various races and regions can only be dimly discerned from the scraps of history which have come down to us. From *The Gododdin* we learn that the men of Gododdin fought against Saxons, Irish and Picts; and, in the intervals, they also fought against other British kingdoms. But the Saxons proved the strongest of all the warring forces, and by the middle of the seventh century, the kingdom of Gododdin had been overrun. An old alliance between the kingdoms of Strathclyde and Dalriada broke down early in the century, and soon after the battle of Chester in 616, the land link between the Welsh and northern kingdoms was broken. Forty years later, when the struggle for the Saxon hegemony was won by Oswy from Penda, the British were allied to Penda; and with this defeat at Winwaed Field in 655, the last chance of reunion with the north vanished.

Despite the decline in Saxon power in Scotland after Ecg-frith's death at Nechtanmere in 685, the Britons there never re-established effective political contact with Wales, though some degree of cultural contact continued. Because it was the Irish kings of Dalriada who finally won the hegemony of Scotland early in the tenth century, the traditions of the Britons of the north, the 'Gwyr y Gogledd', were not preserved there. Such cultural remains as survive have all been handed down through Welsh sources, and the existence of any written records made before the men of the north came to Wales is a matter of conjecture.[4] Since Welsh culture remained largely unrecorded in writing until the thirteenth century, there would have been little more than a bare chronicle or two; the chief sources of Welsh history, the panegyrics and genealogies of the royal houses include a handful of those about the rulers of the north, among them Taliesin's and Aneirin's poems. These seem, as far as we can tell, to have been brought south during the seventh and eighth centuries; some stories about the deeds of their northern cousins must have reached the Welsh before the land link was severed, while others were brought by refugees.

The fact that no poetry from the south has survived from these early centuries suggests – though this can be no more than a theory – that the earliest poetic traditions of north and south were different either in style or quality. Taliesin wrote a eulogy for Cynan Garwyn of Powys, and may have begun his career there; but he found fame at the court of Urien of Rheged.[5]* The only apparently early poems from Powys, attributed to Llywarch the Old, have been shown to belong to the ninth century:[6] they are brilliant evocations of a situation in the seventh century which closely paralleled that in Powys three hundred years later, but the only early part of them is the names of the historical chieftain and his family to whom they are ascribed. The poetry from south Wales is much more concerned with the past, and with heroic figures. It no longer uses current events as its main theme, but continually harks back to an earlier – one is tempted to say golden – age. This is partly due to the changed circumstances in which the poets of the eighth and ninth century worked. There was now little real hope of regaining the lost lands; at best, the Saxons could be held off, but the heroic age was over. The deeds of the past had been woven gradually into connected stories, such as the list of Cadwallawn's battles in the Red Book of Hergest, which is an early form of posthumous memorial, probably an excerpt from a saga in prose and verse such as are found in Irish literature. These sagas seem to have been the property of storytellers as distinct from the official court poets, a distinction which was made formal in the titles of *cyfarwydd*, given to the storyteller, and *bardd*, used of court poets. The work of storyteller and bard

---

* See p. 77 for a relatively early tradition connecting Taliesin and Arthur.

intermingled to some extent: the bard would refer to the same famous heroes whose exploits the storyteller described.

The poetic inheritance from northern Britain had originally contained little except bardic material; by the time it came to be recorded in the early ninth century, it had been worked over by the storytellers and integrated with their local legends and more general myths, as well as with the traditional tales which are the basis of folklore throughout the world. One of the most remarkable features of this adaptation is the way in which heroes from the north are 'placed' in the south. Early Celtic literature is much concerned with names and localities, and to explain a placename a writer will introduce a new episode into a story. Two particularly prominent heroes who moved south in this way were Gwyddno and Drystan mab Tallwch;[7] the latter, linked in very early years with March of Cornwall, becomes in medieval romance Tristan, nephew of King Mark. Such transfers were not made entirely fortuitously, as there is an early memorial to a Drustanus at Castledore in Cornwall, which may have inspired the new location for his namesake's legends.

If, then, the northern tradition is narrowly concerned with present events, and was later elaborated in the south, a reference to an Arthur in *The Gododdin* is unlikely to imply a hero of wide renown from another part of England, but a recent, local character. When a hero from outside the northern British lands appears, he is usually identified as such: *Gereint rac deheu*, 'Geraint from the south', is an example. Here a caveat must be entered: the text of *The Gododdin*, as might be expected from the long chain of transmission by which it reached its present written form, is seriously corrupted. At one point a ninth-century lullaby, 'Dinogad's Petticoat', has been inserted; a delightful piece but totally out of context. At another point we learn of Aneirin's death and how

> Since earth has covered Aneirin
> now song has left the land of Gododdin.[8]

So it is possible that the reference to Arthur is either an inter-polation or a substitution after his legend had become famous. However, the question is sufficiently open to allow us to assume for the moment that the line is original.

We must therefore look for an Arthur in the north more or less contemporary with Aneirin: and a prince of that name does indeed appear, in a literary source very different from the traditions we have been describing. Saint Columba, founder of the monastery at Iona, spent most of his life as a missionary in Scotland, and was a contemporary of Aedan mac Gabrain, ruler of the kingdom of Dalriada in what is now Argyll and Kintyre. Aedan, who had succeeded to the throne about 574, was an energetic king, and in frequent conflict with his neighbours, particularly the Picts to the north and the kingdom of Fortrenn to the east. The relations between Columba and Aedan are recorded in the biography of the former, written by Adomnan, perhaps Abbot of Hy in about 700: that is, about a century after Columba's death. Adomnan describes two prophecies by the saint concerning 'the battle of the Miathi':

At another time, before the above-mentioned battle, the saint questioned king Aidan about a successor to the kingdom. When he answered that he did not know which of his three sons should reign, Artuir, or Echoid Find, or Domingart, the saint then spoke in this manner: 'None of these three will be king; for they will fall in battles, slain by enemies. But now, if you have others that are younger, let them come to me, and the one whom the Lord has chosen from among them to be king will run at once to my knee.'

They were called, according to the saint's word; and when Echoid Buide came in, he leaned on Columba's bosom. Immediately the saint kissed and blessed him, and said to the father: 'This is the survivor, and he will reign after you as king; and his sons will reign after him.'

All these things were completely fulfilled afterwards, in their time. For Artuir and Echoid Find were slain a little while later, in the battle of the Miathi mentioned above. Domingart was killed in a rout of battle in England. And Echoid Buide succeeded to the kingdom after his father.[9]

Remembering that armies were small in those days – compare the three hundred horsemen and perhaps three thousand foot of the Catraeth expedition – this account implies that the 'battle of the Miathi' was hard won, perhaps a major event in Aedan's reign. But we do not know exactly who the Miathi were. They may have been from the borders of the area known as Manau Gododdin; perhaps they are the Maeatae of Dio Cassius, a tribe living just north of the Antonine wall.[10] The battle was sufficiently important to attract the attention of the Irish writers; the Annals of Tigernach record a year after Columba's death (thus contradicting the account of Adomnan), 'the slaying of the sons of Aedan, Bran and Domingert and Eochaid Find and Artur, in the battle of Circhind in which Aedan was victor'.[11] This rather confused report can be explained to some extent by a corresponding entry in the Ulster Annals, which speaks of 'the slaying of the sons of Aedan, Brain and Domangairt'. It would seem that Tigernach has confused an episode in which Bran and Domingart were killed – we know from the Life of St Columba that Domingart was killed 'in the Saxon Lands' – with the battle of the Miathi. To which episode Circhind (or Cercenn) belongs is impossible to say: the place has been tentatively named as either Coupar Angus or Kincardine O'Neil, well to the north of the area of the Maeatae, or perhaps even an area rather than a place, between the Tay and the Dee.[12] A further confusion is introduced by the Pictish king list, *Senchus Fer n Alban*, which gives Arthur as the grandson, not the son, of Aedan, and names Conaing as Aedan's son.

What are we to make of these conflicting reports? Although Adomnan gives the clearest and most circumstantial account, all that can reasonably be taken as clear is that there was a prince named Arthur among Aedan's family, who perished in a hard-won victory against one of the Pictish tribes of the north. He *may* have been the eldest of Aedan's sons, and with such a warlike father, he almost certainly took part in other campaigns besides the one in which he met his death. But, most important of all for our present purpose, he flourished within a mere decade or so in time and a mere fifty miles in space of the milieu in which *The Gododdin* was written. He therefore meets the criterion of a local, contemporary hero of the type celebrated everywhere else in that poem. The reference to him comes from an early and reliable source, which, as we shall see, cannot be said of the rival and generally accepted candidate.

The background of Arthur of Dalriada was Irish: the kingdom had been founded by emigrants from Ireland in about A D 500, under the leadership of Fergus mac Erc. The land which they seized was nominally Pictish, being beyond the wall erected by Antoninus Pius in the second century, and they soon formed common cause with the Britons against the highland tribes. Aedan's reign, however, marks a turning point in the hitherto cordial relations with the British, despite his possible family connections with them.* He has earned the epithet in Welsh legend of *bradawc*, wily or treacherous; and it seems that an alliance of some years' standing with his southern neighbours in Strathclyde came to an end, perhaps because they suspected his territorial ambitions. Not long after the battle of the Miathi, Aedan raided Northumbria, beyond the British part of Scotland, and was defeated at Degsastan, a battle dated by Bede to 603. This expedition shows why the Britons both suspected him and yet were his allies: any prince with sufficient power to dispatch an army against a relatively distant enemy was an uncomfortable neighbour; but Aedan's sympathies remained with the British, and the Degsastan battle may even have been in support of the expedition recorded in *The Gododdin*.[13] At all events, Aedan was clearly remembered in the

* These are often cited as a reason for his having called his son Arthur, after the hypothetical earlier British hero of that name. But this could equally well show that his relations with the British were close enough for them to adopt his son as one of their heroes.

traditions of the Welsh three centuries later, so there is no reason why his son's memory should not have been preserved in the same way, particularly as the actual break with the Britons, if such indeed there was, would seem to have been after Arthur's death. And Aedan's own reputation is no argument against a favourable image of his son in British records. There are, it is true, occasional hostile references to Dalriada in British material, but these all date from after Aedan s reign, and would only serve to enhance Arthur's memory if he had indeed fought on the side of the British, as seems likely.

A faint and distant echo of one of Arthur of Dalriada's adventures may have been preserved in a late eleventh-century *Life of St Gildas*. St Gildas's father, Caw of Pritdin, is said to have lived north of the Antonine wall, therefore not far from the territory of Dalriada; and Arthur appears in the story in a rather unfavourable light:

St Gildas was the contemporary of Arthur, the king of the whole of Britain, whom he loved exceedingly, and whom he always desired to obey. Nevertheless his twenty-three brothers constantly rose up against the afore-mentioned rebellious king (*regi rebelli*), refusing to own him as their lord; but they often routed and drove him out from forest and battlefield. Hueil, the eldest brother, an active warrior and most distinguished soldier, submitted to no king, not even to Arthur. He used to harass the latter, and to provoke the greatest anger between them both. He would often swoop down from Scotland, set up conflagrations, and carry off spoils with victory and renown. In consequence, the king of all Britain, on hearing that the high-spirited youth had done such things, and was doing similar things, pursued the victorious and excellent youth, who, as the inhabitants used to assert and hope, was destined to become king. In the hostile pursuit and council of war held in the island of Minau, he killed the young plunderer. After that murder the victorious Arthur returned, rejoicing greatly that he had overcome his bravest enemy. Gildas, the historian of the Britons, who was staying in Ireland, directing studies and preaching in the city of Armagh, heard that his brother had been slain by king Arthur. He was grieved at hearing the news, wept with lamentation, as a dear brother for a dear brother. He prayed daily for his brother's spirit; and, moreover, he used to pray for Arthur, his brother's persecutor and murderer, fulfilling the apostolic commandment, which says: Love those who persecute you and do good to them that hate you.[14]

If we add the details of this story to that of Caw of Pritdin, Hueil would have been raiding from Pictish territory into Dalriada; and 'the island of Minau' could well be a confusion for Manau Gododdin, the British kingdom in eastern Scotland. Furthermore, we shall see that there may be another confusion over the identity of Gildas, who is perhaps not Gildas the Wise, 'the historian of the Britons', of the mid-sixth century but a later saint of that name. What concerns us for the moment is that we have here another story of a northern Arthur, albeit overlaid with later details, which could have concerned Arthur of Dalriada. It is a very late version of an early story, its long pedigree betrayed by the ambivalent attitude to Arthur, who is branded as '*rex rebellis*' without any reason being given and is obscurely to blame for slaying a troublesome marauder. It is as though an earlier story had told of Gildas's rebellious brothers, Arthur's victory over them, and how Gildas forgave Arthur for doing his duty: but a later editor had tried to whiten the name of Gildas and his family, clumsily blackening Arthur's in the process. Or might it even be some episode in the tradition of Aedan whom the Britons came to call 'the treacherous', a betrayal of an ally by his son? In this case, the epithet would be deserved, and the confusion would be between the primitive Arthur and the later 'ruler of wide lands'.

This, then, is the first of our Arthurian figures: a Scottish chieftain's son of Irish descent, Christian in the Celtic tradition, a leader and warrior who met his death at a relatively early age in a battle against heathen barbarians, somewhere around the end of the sixth century, and attained a small but solid fame in local stories and in the songs of local bards.

3

3 Arthur of Dyfed

For the last century of their occupation of Britain, the Romans were largely concerned with the problem of repelling barbarian attacks on the island, mostly with a view to plunder, and chiefly from the east. The Counts of the Saxon Shore have become figures of popular history, riding furiously from shore station to shore station as the narrow keels of the invaders appeared silently and without warning over the horizon. But this was only one of a group of commands covering the province of Britannia; the north had been a frontier against the Pictish tribes since the earliest years of Roman rule, and we have already looked at the continuing warfare there. The west, however, is rarely mentioned as a defensive coast: the successive movement westwards of Saxons and Danes overshadows the much smaller reverse migration of the Irish raiders of the fourth to seventh centuries.

The obscurity of this movement is increased by the relative closeness of Welsh and Irish culture up to the sixth century AD, and by the Roman preoccupation with a restless native population in Wales. The great fortresses of Segontium (Caernarvon), Maridunum (Carmarthen) and Isca (Caerleon) served to over-awe the latter as much as to provide bases for operations on the coasts: and it is problematical to what degree the Irish were prepared to brave the Roman defences. However, Irish settlements were established in the south-west about the end of the fourth century AD, following the withdrawal of troops by Maximus in 383,[1] particularly in the kingdom of Dyfed or Pembrokeshire.* The distribution of Christian monuments shows a definite orientation towards Ireland from the fifth century onwards: the crosses are grouped clearly on the western

* Some authorities date this invasion to the third century, though accurate calculations are difficult. In what follows, all dates are approximate, on the basis of a fourth-century invasion date.

coasts, while few are found in the areas once occupied by the Romans.

The historical records of the Irish settlement of Dyfed are slight, but give some important details. The invaders were the Déssi, a tribe from Co. Meath, whose history is recorded in a short history *The Expulsion of the Déssi*, dating in its original form to the latter half of the eighth century.[2] The history is chiefly concerned with the wars in Ireland which led to their departure, telling how Cormac mac Airt drove them from Meath into Leinster, where their king was slain; but a brief paragraph tells of their subsequent fate:

Eochaid, son of Artchorp, went over sea with his descendants into the territory of Demed, and it is there that his sons and grandsons died. And from them is the race of Crimthann over there, of which is Tualodor mac* Rigin maic Catacuind maic Caittienn, maic Clotenn maic Naiee maic Artuir maic Retheoir maic Congair maic Gartbuir maic Alchoil maic Trestin maic Aeda Broisc maic Corath maic Echach Almuir maic Arttchuirp.[3]

This agrees very closely, allowing for variations in spelling, with the pedigrees of the rulers of Dyfed preserved in the Welsh genealogies which reads in part:

... Tuedos map* Regin map Catgocaun map Cathen map Clothen map Nougoy map Arthur map Petr map Cincar map Guortepir map Aircol map Triphun map Clotri map Gloitguin map Nimet map Dimet map Maxim Guletic map Protec map Protector map Ebiud map Eliud map Stater map Pincr misser map Constans map Constantini Magni.[4]

The earlier part of the Welsh genealogy is obviously corrupt: 'Dimet' looks like an attempt to explain the name Demed or Dyfed, while the earlier names are duplicated, with a Roman title and a Roman coin offered as proper names, and the obligatory great progenitor in the shape of Constantine the

* Mac, maic, map = son of.

Great! Although attempts have been made to reconcile the two conflicting accounts,[5] too much ingenuity is needed to explain away the Welsh version, while the Irish pedigree seems coherent and reasonably acceptable.

Given that the Déssi moved westwards after Maximus's withdrawal of the legions in 383 – and this can be no more than an assumption – we would arrive at a date of about 580–620 for the birth of Arthur of Dyfed: unfortunately the only piece of supporting evidence, a supposedly seventh-century charter of his son Nouy, is almost certainly a twelfth-century forgery, so the rough and ready method of 'thirty years to a generation' is all we can use. The date itself is not crucial; what is far more important is that we have evidence of a second Arthur of Irish origins in an area where Arthurian traditions were to become particularly strong, at a very similar period to Arthur of Dalriada.

The name Arthur continues to be very rare until the twelfth century. There are only two other examples in the seventh century; and both again have connections either with Ireland or the Irish kingdoms. About 620–625, an entry in the Annals of Tigernach records that 'Mongan mac Fiachna Lurgan was struck with a stone by Artuir son of Bicoir the Briton and died'. A verse follows:

> Cold is the wind over Islay;
> there are warriors in Kintyre,
> they will commit a cruel deed therefor,
> they will kill Mongan, son of Fiachna.[6]

This could be taken to imply that Artuir was one of the warriors in Kintyre, within the kingdom of Dalriada; and in any case the context implies not war between Irish and Britons, but a purely private quarrel, which would also put Artuir into an Irish context, that of Mongan and his followers. The last of the seventh-century Arthurs is also a shadowy figure, grandfather of the priest Feradach who signed a charter with Adomnan, author of the *Vita Columbae*, in 697. He could be Arthur of Dalriada himself, but in any case probably belonged to the same area and background.

Against this very clear evidence of a group of Arthurs appearing in an early Irish context, implying an Irish origin for the name, there are no Welshmen of the same name until we come to ninth-century records. But there are other candidates for our attention, from a very different background. Artorius is a rare, but by no means unknown Roman name, the name of a small *gens* or family group. Nine or ten members of this group appear in prominent positions in the Empire, chiefly in the first and second centuries.[7] A C. Artorius Proculus held the senatorial office of Rhetor in 352; but there is a much more interesting figure among them.[8] L. Artorius Castus is commemorated on two monuments near Split in Yugoslavia. He seems to have been a member of a branch of the Artorian *gens* settled in that neighbourhood, and he had a distinguished military career, beginning in the East, where he may have taken part in the Jewish campaign of AD 132–135. He later commanded the fleet off Misenum; but the most interesting part of his career was his appointment as *praefectus* of the legion VI Victrix, stationed at York. During his command here, he was sent on a special expedition to Brittany to suppress a rebellion there, as general commanding a mixed force of legionaries and auxiliaries. This was his last spell of active service, and he held a high civil post at the time when the longer of the two inscriptions was cut.

Any connection between Lucius Artorius Castus and the Irish and Welsh Arthurs must be extremely tenuous. We can only conjecture that distant memories of L. Artorius Castus's campaigns, perhaps stray inscriptions on Roman sites, might have encouraged later writers to embellish the legend of Arthur in otherwise unsuspected ways. To build a bridge of tradition from second-century Roman Britain to ninth-century Wales with no other support is a daring feat of imagination, but not admissible evidence. Nor are the 'coincidences' such as L. Artorius Castus's Breton expedition and the idea of an overseas expedition by the mythical Arthur any stronger than the supposed links between the Roman general and the occasional use of the name Artor near York in the eleventh century recorded in Domesday Book. It might be possible to derive a Welsh use of the name Arthur from the Roman *gens* Artorius by way of the Romano-British leaders of the late fifth century; but again our evidence so far has shown an Irish background for the early Arthurs, with the probability that it was an Irish name. The evidence for an Arthur with a Welsh background is our next problem.

4 The Unknown Leader: Badon Hill

So far, the records we have used have been sparse in the extreme, the dry bones of memory. When we turn to the Welsh traditions about Arthur we are confronted by works which have the flesh and blood of a long tradition about them: and in order to weigh them up we must look briefly at that tradition.

History in the early Middle Ages can be very broadly divided into three streams: the celebration of heroes (as in *The Gododdin*), the recording of great events (as in the Irish annals) and the search for a moral to be drawn from the apparent confusion of the world. The celebration of heroes is the most primitive form of history, and the epic flourishes best in the absence of written history. These oral poems are the most difficult materials of all to use, as they are rarely straightforward, rarely concerned with details of time and place, and all too liable to enthusiastically exaggerate the deeds of the central figure. On the other hand, they can be transmitted from generation to generation with surprising accuracy, as the survival of the *Iliad* with its clear geography of the Aegean and of Troy shows; and Serbian epics collected in this century have recorded fifteenth-century events with similarly correct details. But the early Welsh heroic poems are less easy to use as history: they do not even trouble with what happened, but only with who did it. The hero's glory is everything, the causes and consequences nothing.

Annals, too, although apparently more promising, have their pitfalls as well. The word *annals* was taken over from Roman historians, who had used it in a much more complex sense: Tacitus's *Annals* are not year-by-year entries, but a complex narrative. The simpler yearly entries of the early medieval monks derive from a different need, that of recording the passage of years in order to calculate the feasts of the Church correctly.

The basis of many such records were the tables of Easter, drawn up on the Continent in the third and fourth centuries AD as the Church's growing power made an increasing degree of organization necessary. Unfortunately, the issue was confused by local variations in chronology, partly due to misunderstanding of the Roman system of reckoning from the founding of Rome (*ab urbe condita*, or AUC) in 753 BC.

It was not until the Synod of Whitby in 664, at which the Celtic Church was reconciled with Roman use, that the system of dating from the birth of Our Lord was first employed as a means for giving dates, and the idea was not a copy of Continental practice but an innovation of the English bishop Wilfrid. Both earlier and later Celtic records use varying starting points, year 1 sometimes being no more than the year in which a particular set of annals was started. The information they contain is also extremely sparse, though it is all too easy to look at a modern transcription of an early annal, and take its bald statements against a particular date as being solidly based facts. We shall return to this problem in connection with the *Annales Cambriae* (Annals of Wales), where a long and obscure passage gives the starting date in the fifth century, from which the years of the annal are reckoned. And there is the further complication that even quite early records may have been compiled from two sets of records incorrectly collated by the compiler, so that a mixture of correct dates and errors results.

By contrast, the difficulties presented by moralistic history are more obvious, but they can be equally frustrating. In the ancient world, the figure of Homer cast a long shadow over both poetry and history: in the first century AD Quintilian remarked that 'history is very near to poetry and may be considered in some sense as poetry in prose'.[1] Herodotus and Thucydides are dramatic writers, with an eye for a great set piece; and they adopt the very theatrical convention of summarizing attitudes or situations by means of a fictitious speech delivered by a key figure in the action, a device which was to give a false immediacy to history throughout the Middle Ages. And as with the Athenian playwrights, there is an underlying concern with the moral implication of the events they portray.

With the triumph of Christianity, new dimensions were added to the historian's attitude. The Old Testament was a prelude to man's redemption, the hand of God in man's affairs. Furthermore, the idea of typology came to dominate historical thinking: everything in the Old Testament prefigured something in the New Testament and its consequences, just as everything on the land was supposed by medieval thinkers to have its equivalent form in the sea. So the context of historical writing was the Bible: it became a kind of modern supplement to biblical events, drawn in prophetic terms. Just as the biblical past foreshadowed the present, so the present was also the key to the future.

The early Christians had not been greatly concerned with history after the writing of the Acts of the Apostles in the first century AD; for the young Church lived in hourly expectation of the Second Coming. It was only after the acceptance of Christianity as the official imperial religion in the fourth century that the first Christian history, Eusebius's *Ecclesiastical History*, appeared. Given the circumstances, it is scarcely surprising that the author, friend and confidant of Constantine, is more interested in justifying Christianity's new pact with Imperial Rome, the Rome that her preachers had so often denounced as the empire that should precede the coming of Antichrist, than in giving a purely factual account. Constantine and his predecessors became part of the pattern of divine providence: the peace established by Augustus is a necessary prelude to the incarnation, because in peaceful conditions it was easier to spread the Gospel message. And just as the Roman Empire was retrospectively incorporated into the scheme of things, so Roman civilization was laid under contribution as well: Virgil's Fourth Eclogue, with its vision of the Golden Age, became a prophecy of Christ's coming: 'Now the Virgin returns, the years of Saturn's rule return; a new first-born is sent down by high heaven, born in the shape of a boy who shall end the Iron Race and resurrect the Golden Age throughout the world.'

From such material as this, Orosius, writing in the fifth century, shaped an even more powerfully Christian view of history, telling Rome's past as though it was a search for salvation like that of Israel. His Roman history provides a precedent for national histories in the period before Christ, showing that such subjects are legitimate studies for the Christian writer by means of an attitude best summed up by the German playwright Kleist: 'The history of the world is the judgement of the world.' Not only does the past of a nation determine its fate at the Day of Judgement, but it also prefigures its future, just as Israel's history prefigured Christian history. And furthermore, secular events could foreshadow spiritual changes; Caesar's empire became an earthly presage of Christ's rule. So, despite Augustine's vision of the 'two cities' which firmly separated heaven and earth, the prevailing attitude among early medieval writers plundered all available sources of the past to preach the doom which, for five centuries, the Church had awaited as imminent.

This exploration of historians' attitude in the late Roman Empire may seem to have little to do with the figure of Arthur, but because we rely on a writer within this tradition for the nearest contemporary account of the period, these are the premises of any attempt to understand his work. Gildas's *On the Ruin of Britain* is not an attempt at a reasoned account of his times: it is Orosius's method transformed into a brilliant vitriolic diatribe on the wickedness of all things British and the virtue of all things Roman. It is a sermon, obscure, learned and immensely difficult to read, almost as though the writer's pen were choked with the fury of his words. Only a brief summary can really convey what this hybrid book contains.

The title means 'On the destruction of Britain', and Gildas himself describes it in the opening sentence as 'this letter, made more in tears than in denunciation'. He makes it clear that this is to be a work of admonition, written after long qualms of conscience, and warns that 'it is not so much my purpose to narrate the dangers of savage warfare incurred by brave soldiers, as to tell of the dangers caused by indolent men'. Before he launches into his sermon proper, however, he says

Let me attempt to say a little, God willing, of the geography, the obstinacy, the conquest and rebellion of our country; and of its reconquest and harsh servitude; of religion, persecution and holy martyrs, of various heresies, of tyrants, of two nations which laid it waste; of its defence and renewed laying waste; of its second revenge and third laying waste, of famine, letters to Agitius, victory, crimes, sudden news of enemies, the famous plague, conferences, enemies far fiercer than the first, the ruin of cities, the survivors, and of the final victory of our country which God's will has granted in our own times.[2]

This rhetorical list does not lead us to expect a very coherent account, nor do we get one. Gildas devotes twenty-four chapters to this prefatory history, beginning from the Roman invasion, often narrated in a pseudo-classical historic present, as if to bring the events more vividly before our eyes. Up to chapter 18, the departure of the Romans, he has Orosius as his guide, and his story is reasonably factual underneath the rhetoric; he has added a few items of local Christian tradition. His chronology is not always certain, and he seems to date the building of Hadrian's Wall more than two hundred years too late.

Once the Romans have left, his outline becomes scanty in the extreme. He speaks first of a renewed invasion of the Scots and Picts and the desertion of the cities (ch. 19) and of an appeal to

the Consul Agitius (Aetius) (ch. 20); but then begins an attack
on the sinfulness of the British leaders (chs 21–22), punished by
renewed Pictish attacks and a great plague, leading up to the
invitation to the Saxons to come and repel the northern tribes.
Of this Gildas tells us that they were invited by 'a proud
tyrant' and that they arrived on the eastern shore in three keels
(*cyulae*). A highly dramatic account of the Saxon ravages
follows, again without tangible facts in it, other than an implication that the Saxons reached the west coast; and the whole
rather sketchy history is brought up to date with a page of
relatively detailed material (chs 25–26):

After some interval, when the cruel ravagers had returned home,
the remnants, strengthened by God, and their numbers swelled by
unhappy citizens from all parts and every side, gathering as eagerly
as a hive of bees when a storm threatens, praying to the Lord with
their whole heart and, as they say, 'burdening the air with innumer-
able prayers' that they should not be slaughtered, take up arms and
challenge their conquerors to battle. Ambrosius Aurelianus was their
leader, a modest man, who alone of the Roman race survived the
shock of these storms (his parents, undoubtedly of the purple, had
been slain in them); nowadays his offspring have in our times
declined from the integrity of their ancestors. To their lot, by the
Lord's favour, there fell the victory.
   From that time onward now the citizens, now the enemy were
victorious, so that the Lord might test in this people the Israel of
today, whether it loves him or not; until the year of the siege of
Mons Badonicus, almost the most recent and not the least slaughter
of these gallows-birds, which also begins the forty-fourth year (as I
know), with one month now elapsed; it is also that of my birth.
But not even now are the cities of our country inhabited as before;
deserted and dismantled, they still lie neglected, for though foreign
wars are at an end, civil wars continue. The recollection of the
desperate slaughter in the island and the unlooked-for help has
remained fixed in the memory of those who witnessed both marvels
and survived; and for this reason kings, public officials, private
persons, priests and clergy all preserved their own rank. As they
died, an age ignorant of that storm followed, acquainted only with

the present calm; all the guiding influences of truth and justice have
been shaken and overturned; so that no recollection, not even a
trace of them is to be found in the aforesaid ranks, save among a
few, few indeed, who because of the departure of that great multitude which rushes headlong to hell each day, are of so small a
number that the venerable Mother Church does not observe them,
her only true children, as they rest in her bosom.[3]

With a last nod to the few virtuous men remaining, Gildas
now launches into his diatribe. Here his rolling periods, like
the waves of some storm-lashed sea of wrath, come into their
own, as he takes on something of a prophet's exaltation:
'Britain has kings, but they are tyrants; judges, but they are
impious men . . .' His flotsam and jetsam of facts is difficult to
recover from the depths of his rhetoric. He denounces the
private sins as much as, if not more than, the public misdeeds
of the five princes, Constantine of Devon, Aurelius Caninus,
Vortipor of Dyfed (great-grandfather of Arthur of Dyfed),
Cuneglasus, and, most powerful of all, Maelgwn of Gwynedd
or north Wales. To the end of denouncing them more thor-
oughly, he first catalogues their sins and then goes through the
Old Testament prophets, extracting the most appropriate
passages, as if his own thunder were not adequate to the task.
And finally he directs a tirade of similar construction against
the members of his own class, the clergy. These two lengthy
diatribes occupy thirty-seven and forty-seven chapters respec-
tively, and offer little historical evidence of any kind.

The first key to Gildas's remarkable capacity for pessimism,
beyond his role as self-appointed scourge of an evil time, is his
hatred for everything that is native to Britain and his admiration
of the golden Roman past. Ambrosius Aurelianus, the saviour
of the island, is represented as the only surviving Roman, as
though only the greatest heroes could possibly be of that race.
The natives are 'treacherous', 'crafty foxes', in their moments of
power, but more often, before the Saxon onslaught, 'lambs' or

'timid fowl'. Yet despite this admiration for all things Roman, he was almost certainly not Roman himself. We have already seen that a very late biography attributes to him a Pictish background, an unlikely starting point for an admirer of Rome. Indeed, this *Life* has led some writers to revive a medieval tradition that there were two Gildases, the writer or *Gildas Badonicus* and the Pictish saint, *Gildas Albanius*. Furthermore, one writer on early Celtic history[4] persistently argued that *On the Ruin of Britain* fell into two parts, the historical section (1–26), written about 700, and the 'Epistle' (27–110), written before 502. However, like the multiple Homers who once flourished in classical scholarship, the dual Gildas and the two parts of his book have not been generally accepted. There is certainly no internal contradiction between the two parts of a kind which would support this idea, since both are equally wanting in names and places. A forger would almost certainly have supplied names and dates to make his work appear authentic; and for two genuine pieces of different periods to coincide so closely is almost impossible. The very idiosyncrasies of Gildas's style that tantalize the historian are the proof of his authenticity.

A little of the general atmosphere in which Gildas was writing can be reconstructed from other sources. The kings whom he decries flourished in the second quarter of the sixth century AD; Maelgwn is said to have died in 547, according to the *Annals of Wales* (though this work, too, presents chronological problems), and Gildas himself in 570. Allowing for discrepancies in dating, Gildas's work is of the period 520–560, that is, over a century after the effective end of the Roman occupation in the early fifth century, and more than fifty years after the arrival of the first Saxon settlers. He was writing in almost total isolation from the Continent, and Irish missionaries whose work in Britain was to dominate the later Celtic Church had not yet begun to cross the Irish Sea. He stands therefore at a crossroads of ecclesiastical history, the moment when the British Church was genuinely independent. If his tremendous indictment of the British clergy has any truth in it, it is easy to see why the British Church did not develop a real spiritual energy of its own. This isolation meant that he had no access to sources of information in Gaul or Ireland, or even outside his own immediate circle. The five princes he decries all belong to Wales and the south-west; there is no word as to the Britons of the north. Above all, he moves in a narrow world, a world of restricted communications. The routes of contact with Gaul by which St Germanus had come to Britain in the mid-fifth century were closed by the Saxon invaders, despite the settlement of Brittany by Celtic peoples at around this period.

We might infer from this almost oppressive isolation that Gildas was working at a time when the Britons of the west had lost their accustomed routes of communication, the old Roman roads of the midlands and south running up to York and the wall, and this concentration on the 'central Britons' is even more curious when we recall that his biographer in the eleventh century made him north British by birth, and says that he went on a mission to Ireland and ended his life an exile in Brittany. Yet nowhere in *On the Ruin of Britain* is there any suggestion from the author that he is not speaking about the whole of British civilization.

The idea of the British nation of the period as a series of isolated communities is further reinforced by linguistic evidence showing that Cornish (and Breton) began to diverge from Welsh proper 'not long after the first Saxon settlements',[5] though Breton did not become distinct until the end of the sixth century. Furthermore, the Church and the few educated nobles outside it were marked off by another distinction, that of using Latin. The bulk of the British population had never learnt Latin, and any Latin-speakers were almost certainly refugees from the Lowland Zone now occupied by the Saxons. (This might explain the absence of Latin literature from the British kingdoms of the north, and likewise Gildas's lack of information about them: refugees from the south and east were more likely to have sought shelter in the west, and the north may have simply lacked Latin speakers and writers.)

The society in which Gildas moved was therefore introspective, and the possibility that he was a monk would increase his isolation. He drew on the past for most of his material: hence the vast tracts of biblical quotation, and perhaps, too, the idea of himself as a 'voice crying in the wilderness'. His inheritance from the continental Church was threefold: first, parts of the Bible in the revision made by St Jerome at the beginning of the fifth century; secondly, some historical works written by ecclesiastics; and thirdly, brief materials on saints' legends and biographies, such as the *passio* of St Alban. Yet Christianity was well established in Britain: Gildas never breathes a word of paganism, only of lack of respect for the accepted Christian standards. So he is set apart by his greater learning, not by his belief: indeed, he assumes that his audience are familiar with the whole of Christian teaching, perhaps as a result of the intense propaganda which had accompanied the battle over the Arian heresies in the previous century: one of the leaders in this learned theological warfare had been the British heretic Pelagius. Hence it is possible that Gildas's book may belong to a native tradition of polemics, carried on among a small, learned circle. The fierceness of his rhetoric is almost certainly a Celtic trait, as there is evidence of rhetorical speaking and writing in Gaul and Ireland from the same period, derived from a deep-rooted pagan tradition.[6]

With this in mind, we can now turn to the brief glimpse of British history at the end of the fifth century which Gildas affords us in the passage already quoted. It is easy to assume that the respite from the Saxons was a general one, and that

Badon Hill was a victory of epic proportions, won by a newly revived British military machine. But a closer examination of Gildas's narrative shows that this was not necessarily the case. First, there is no reason to assume that the respite from the Saxons was more than a local one. Gildas's horizon is limited to the south and south-west, and we cannot assume that Badon Hill was so decisive that the Saxon raids ceased throughout Britain. He does not even imply that part of the island remained in Saxon hands, speaking of the desolate cities as though they were all in British territory. Secondly, there is nothing in his account to deny that Ambrosius Aurelianus could have been the commander throughout the campaigns and even the victor of Badon Hill. The demarcation of time is exceedingly confused throughout the passage. At best, the following divisions can be distinguished:

1. A period of general devastation, lasting 'a certain length of time'.
2. Retreat of the Saxons, followed by a British revival, leading to a period of conflicting fortunes, up to the siege of Badon Hill.
3. Period of peace with the Saxons and of civil wars.

There are only two indications of the length of time which elapsed during these changes. Ambrosius Aurelianus is clearly dead at the time at which Gildas is writing, and his offspring (perhaps first or second generation) 'have greatly degenerated from their ancestral nobleness'. The other passage, involving the date of writing and (perhaps) the date of Badon Hill, is too obscure to allow any definite interpretation. The details which follow imply that sufficient time has elapsed for a revival of the cities, which has however failed to materialize, and for a generation who were 'ignorant of the storm' to come to power; both of which would favour the idea that Gildas was writing forty-four years after Badon Hill. Bede, however, using a manuscript considerably older than any that now survive, connected the year with the 'rascally crew' of Saxons making it their forty-fourth in Britain. This in turn involves us in the hoary debate as to the year of the *Adventus Saxonum*. Gildas's rhetoric has once again so obscured his meaning (or so confused a copyist) that he can tell us nothing of value. We have the name of a battle and the name of a commander, a broad idea of a retreat by the Saxons, perhaps local, perhaps general, followed by civil war. The rest is confusion.

Yet we must look a little further into this obscure period, partly because some writers have chosen to evade the difficulties of connecting Arthur with Badon Hill by labelling the British resurgence 'the Arthurian fact', as though the deeds proved the man's existence. On Gildas's evidence, it would be more reasonable to call it 'the Ambrosian fact'; and here again, some writers have tried to identify Ambrosius and Arthur, despite Ambrosius's clearly distinct personality in later Welsh tradition as 'Emrys Wledig'. Another ingenious identification which makes Gildas conceal Arthur as 'the bear' has also been produced; this assumes that in the passage about Cuneglasus, one of the five tyrants, Gildas is reproaching him with his allegiance to Arthur: 'thou bear, rider of many, and driver of the chariot of the bear's den'.[7] The appellation bear would be a play on Arcturus, the star in the constellation Ursa Major, a phrase which occurs in a passage of the Latin poet Claudian which Gildas probably knew.[8] Both these identifications are pure conjecture, and depend on the assumption that Gildas was deliberately suppressing Arthur's name.

Gildas's account does not necessarily support the idea that Badon Hill was a victory of overwhelming and decisive proportions. We have already pointed out Gildas's limited range of vision, and furthermore he quite clearly states that the Saxon retreat *preceded* the British resurgence: 'When the cruel ravagers *had* returned home . . . the remnant . . . take up arms and challenge their conquerors to battle.' This suggests, not a headlong confrontation, but the harassment of a retreating enemy. Is it possible that the Saxons withdrew for reasons other than military defeat, *before* the Britons began to counterattack? Archaeology and other sources may provide some clues. The pattern of Gildas's story is borne out by archaeological evidence: an initial rapid success, followed by a pause or retreat. The line of penetration in this first period of invasion is not clearly defined, and there are conflicting views as to the interpretation of the evidence; but it is broadly true to say that the Thames valley and the land to the south of it, as well as East Anglia and the south midlands, were occupied. There may have been pockets of British survivors in the wilder parts, such as the Weald of Sussex and the Fens, but the richest and most fertile lands of England fell into Saxon hands. Outside this lowland region, there is little evidence of their penetration; if they made forays into the uplands, they did not hold land there for any length of time. This area also corresponds to the river basins draining to the south and east; like the Vikings after them, they may have used these as lines of communication. There is therefore some evidence to show that the invasion of the Saxons stopped at a natural frontier, a theory which is reinforced if we look at the original reasons for their inroads. The people we call by the generic name Saxon consisted of several tribes: Angles, Jutes and Saxons proper. Their homelands were in northern Germany, Denmark and the North Sea coast, and population increase both there and in central Europe had led to pressure on territory and a shortage of suitable land. Hence the coastal tribes had been driven first to a life of plunder and then to a search for new lands. There was obviously a limit to their needs, and it is quite possible that the original pressures which led to the invasion of Britain had run out of impetus when they came up against this first natural obstacle. They had plundered the richest quarter of Britain; and before real settlement began,

they turned their attention to other territory ripe for the pluck-
ing. There is evidence of the presence of Saxons from Britain
in the upper Rhine valley. When the pressures on the Saxon
homelands were renewed, a fresh wave of invaders arrived,
about 570, who moved north and west into the uplands, and
the second retreat of the Britons began.

In the absence of decisive evidence, such a reading of British
history from 470–570 must remain conjecture. But it is at least
as plausible an interpretation of Gildas as the idea of a sudden
British military revival. The ingenious attempts to explain such
a revival by the use of new tactics and especially of cavalry are
so much romance. There is a total lack of archaeological or
other evidence to support the idea of a force of mounted British
soldiers at this period. Cavalry were not a particularly effective
weapon against footsoldiers, and the much quoted Byzantine
cataphracts or heavily armed horsemen were not particularly
distinguished by their successes. The defeat of the Byzantine
armies at Adrianople in 378 by the Goth horsemen was due as
much to tactical mistakes as to the different types of army.
Above all, horses were still for the most part unshod, and the
riders had no stirrups. Both these innovations date from the
seventh century or later in Britain, and horsemen could neither
travel long distances over rough terrain nor charge effectively.
Furthermore, the native breed of horses were small-boned,
ponies rather than chargers; even as a means of transport, they
would have been little faster over long distances than footsoldiers.

So Badon Hill is unlikely to have been won by a kind of
primitive forerunner of knightly cavalry: it is also possible that
it may not have been a concerted Saxon attack on a British fort,
as is usually assumed. It is equally likely that a Saxon band of
marauders could have pitched camp in one of the old Iron Age
hill forts, and have been surrounded and slaughtered by the
British. Once again, this would subtly alter the perspective:

instead of a British resistance to an invading and besieging Saxon horde, Badon Hill could be no more than the liquidation of a small band which found itself outnumbered. Again, there is no way of choosing between the two theories, but the possibility remains that Badon Hill was not such a decisive moment as Gildas's haphazard narrative makes it appear.

Finally, ignoring for a moment the quagmires of disputed chronology and accepting the most common dating for Gildas, that he was born about 500, wrote *On the Ruin of Britain* before 547, and died about 570, we are left with an undoubted gap between Ambrosius Aurelianus, who would seem to belong to the third quarter of the fifth century, and even as victor of Badon Hill would figure no later than AD 500, and the tyrants against whom Gildas rages. There is at least one generation where we have no leader's name, and very little idea of what was happening. History abhors a vacuum; but there is no logical reason for filling it with the name of a hero whose historical origins are obscure. Gildas tells us that 'kings, public officials, private persons, priests, ecclesiastics, severally preserved their own rank'; the miraculous easing of the Saxon pressure produced a hierarchy, a hierarchy better than that of his own day. But his phrase almost contradicts the idea of one outstanding leader. It was a later age, looking to such a leader for victory against the same Saxon hordes, that supplied the missing, mystical figure, so that the memory of his triumphant past could inspire present success.

5 The Bardic Image: Names and Places

To the Celtic mind, names of people and places had a strange fascination of their own. One of the chief functions of the Irish storytellers was the explanation of the significance of place names; and the Welsh bards were responsible for memorizing the long traditional genealogies, which record only the barest outline of descent. But this apparently dry learning fulfilled an important function in a society where the written word was unknown except for the Church's Latin records. It provided the bare bones of history, an endless series of mnemonics on which the bard could build his repertoire, either of comparisons used in praising his patrons or of stories and legends. Place names reflected quite recent and real events, and were likewise a key to the past; and in a highly conservative society the same materials were in continuous use for several centuries.

This transmission of names was usually accurate, in so far as we can check it. But because almost all secular literature depended on the themes prompted by these names, there was a tendency for gradual shifts of emphasis to occur: an explanation for a place name would be invented, a story would be transferred from a minor hero to a major one. Fashion might dictate such a change: stories about a popular hero would be more in demand than those about obscure figures, and the bard could always supplement his stock by a discreet change of name. The process is at its most evident in late records, where Arthur's ascendant fame has enabled him to oust numerous earlier heroes.

The records which the bards preserved by word of mouth were written down from the ninth century onwards: most of the surviving versions are from the twelfth century or later. They fall into two main groups, the genealogies already mentioned and the triads. The triads, groups of three heroes or famous objects or events with a common attribute, are a curious literary form whose origins may go back to the pre-Roman period. They were originally mnemonic, but may have been used in their present form as a means of drawing on an audience to ask for more stories.[1] If this theory be correct, a bard might end one of his stories of Arthur's exploits: 'For Arthur was one of the Three Red Ravagers of the Isle of Britain.' This would be the cue for his audience to ask: 'Who were the other Red Ravagers?', to which the bard would reply: 'There were three Red Ravagers of the Isle of Britain: Arthur, and Rhun son of Beli, and Morgant the Wealthy.'[2] The genealogies are not our modern complex family trees, but groups of single lines of descent, usually designed to connect a prince and his house to a famous ancestor. So they are not exclusively in the male line: at the critical point, the mother's line may be introduced. The pedigree of Arthur of Dyfed already quoted (p. 35) is one example; another is that of the great-grandson of Rhodri the Great, the ninth-century ruler of Gwynedd, a family to whom we shall return: 'Owen son of Iguel son of Catell son of Rotri (Rhodri) son of Mermin, son of Etthil, daughter of Cinnau son of Rotri son of Iutgaul son of Catgualart son of Catgollaun son of Catman son of Jacob son of Beli son of Run son of Mailcun . . . ' and so on through eighteen generations to 'Amalech, who was son of Beli the Great, and Anna his mother, who, they say, was cousin to the Virgin Mary, mother of our Lord Jesus Christ.'[3]

As one might expect, the genealogies are reasonably accurate in their more recent account of each family. But their earlier sections are governed to a large extent by certain formal needs, above all that of tracing back the family to a recognized heroic figure: the legendary pre-Roman ruler Beli the Great, the emperors Constantine and Maximus, the early Welsh princes, Cunedda and Coel the Old (our 'Old King Cole'). The purpose of this material was deliberate propaganda, to enhance the standing of the prince concerned. Of these five figures, the literary tradition knew relatively little about Beli Mawr and

Coel the Old, while Cunedda appears largely as a 'great progenitor' in saintly biographies. Constantine (Custennin) and Maximus (Maxen Wledig) only appear in relatively late triads. The early poets mention only Coel Hen, but again he is a shadowy ancestor-figure. Beli may have owed his prominence to a corrupt text of the fourth-century historian Orosius, whose work Gildas knew. The Roman historian Suetonius speaks of 'Adminius, son of Cynobellinus King of the Britains',[4] who surrendered to Caligula in Germany in AD 40; Orosius makes him into 'Minocynobellinus', who reappears as 'Bellinus . . . [who] was son of Minocannus' in Nennius's *History of the Britons*. On the other hand, both this figure and Beli Mawr may represent a dim memory of the Celtic god Belenus; Bran son of Llyr is another figure of mythological origin who entered the genealogies.

It would seem probable that the earlier parts of the genealogies are in fact the latest additions, made in the ninth or tenth centuries, shortly before the texts were probably written down for the first time; and there is a distinct antiquarian air about them. Figures such as Constantine are rediscoveries, not part of the original tradition, added by scholars with a wider knowledge of the Roman past than their bardic predecessors.

The more recent part of the genealogies, in the form in which they have come down to us, fulfilled a mere practical function.[5] The *Laws of Hywel Dda* in the tenth century reflect a tribal society in Wales where relationships and blood ties were of the utmost importance, not only, as in Anglo-Saxon England, because of the legal responsibility of the family for the actions of all its members, but also because Welsh society was strongly hierarchical, and a man's standing in the eyes of the law depended on his ancestry. At the head were the privileged *cenheddloed*, of royal blood, with special privileges, to whom the genealogies relate. Below them were an indistinct series of ranks, each with their own legal status, most clearly reflected in the differing payments for *galanas* or compensation for culpable homicide. The Anglo-Saxon system differed in that rank was less dependent on ancestry, whether derived from wealth or from royal or local office: and from a very early date the Anglo-Saxon legal system relied extensively on written records.

When the Welsh genealogies came to be recorded, the copyists frequently failed to understand their material. Reduplications are frequent, causing the same person or persons to appear twice, and abbreviations were sometimes misunderstood. The classic instance was pointed out by George Owen Harry as early as 1604:

Of this *Beli Mawr*, or Beli the Great, most of our ancient Brittish Genealogies take their originall, as a chief roote, whereof grew that toy, that the Welsh men derive their pedegrees from the blessed Virgin *Mary*, because in Our Genealogies, this name is met often with B.M. which in deede is *Beli Mawr* and not *Beata Maria*.[6]

So the genealogy of Rhodri Mawr's house quoted earlier ends with a mythical king who also doubles as the Virgin Mary. Nonetheless, this unreliability of the early parts of the genealogies should not blind us to the value of the remainder. As a broad rule, they are potentially reliable for about twenty generations back from 1200, though on occasions there has been later interference.

In all this Arthur plays no part of any substance, except in the Dyfed genealogy which parallels *The Expulsion of the Déssi*. There are about half a dozen references to him in late manuscripts, but only the Dyfed genealogy appears in the earliest group in the all-important British Museum MS Harleian 3859. Collections using twelfth-century material have various versions of Arthur's pedigree, based on the earliest fictional history of him, Geoffrey of Monmouth's *History of the Kings of Britain*. A sixteenth-century manuscript[7] produces another genealogy based on the story of Culhwch and Olwen, and there are other occasional variations designed to make him ancestor or cousin of a saint; he appears as uncle of St David in Geoffrey of Monmouth. Not all of this weaving of historical castles in the air may be as late as it appears; there is good evidence from the lives of the Welsh saints that the process began in the eleventh century. But what is most remarkable is that so few pedigrees include Arthur. Beli Mawr, Cunedda and Coel Hen, Constantine and Maximus are accepted, Arthur is not. It would seem on the face of it that his fame must belong to a period later than that at which the genealogies were recorded, and hence to some extent fixed, which would also explain why his appearances can so frequently be identified at once as later intrusions. Can it be that Arthur has almost no place in earlier Welsh tradition?

The triads present complex problems of interpretation. The chief difficulty is that they are formulas from an oral literature, handed down by word of mouth and recited in public, which have been recorded in written form by scribes who did not necessarily understand their nature. The general outline of the change from oral to written literature is gradually becoming clearer, thanks to the patient work of scholars. From the almost entirely spoken forms of the ninth century, writing plays an increasingly important part until it is a generally accepted medium in the early thirteenth century. This is not to say that poets did not continue to recite their poems; the change was in the long-term transmission of their work, which, despite the vagaries of medieval scribes, now took on a much more rigid form. The contest between the recited romances, or *chwedleu*, and their written counterparts is sharply underlined by the author of *The Dream of Rhonabwy* of the early twelfth century, who bids his reader farewell in the following words:

And this story is called the Dream of Rhonabwy. And here is the reason why no one, neither bard nor storyteller, knows the Dream without a book – by reason of the number of colours that were on the horses, and all that variety of rare colours both on the arms and their trappings, and on the precious mantles, and the magic stones.[8]

But the romance form itself is far distant from the heroic poetry of *The Gododdin*. There are therefore two earlier developments to be accounted for before we reach the literary milieu of *The Dream of Rhonabwy*: the passage from heroic poetry to recited romances, and the change from recital to writing. Heroic poetry tends in its simplest form to be concerned with immediate events and local heroes. A certain length of tradition is required before the epic poem, telling the story of the hero, becomes current. Heroic poetry assumes that the audience knew what the outcome of the battle was, and is concerned with individual feats; the context is of little importance. Epic poems only become attractive as a form when the audience needs to be told who the heroes were.

The historical circumstances of the early British poets meant that, although their society was comparatively advanced, conditions were not right for the epic form. When Aneirin composed *The Gododdin*, it was a little more than a century since the British had ceased to think of themselves as subjects of the Roman empire. This psychological break was a sharp one; Gildas outlines the division at its most decisive: and there were therefore no heroic figures of sufficiently dim antiquity to encourage epic rather than heroic memorials. *Romanitas* was soon equated with Christianity, not with Classical Roman culture, and it is in this role that later Welsh poetry remembers the Roman emperors as forerunners and progenitors. Other classical references were the work of later generations consciously delving into their past, not of a continuously-memorised tradition from Roman times to the Middle Ages. The epic period, which Irish storytellers, their cultural tradition unbroken by the Romans, had already reached, therefore appeared in early Welsh literature during the seventh and eighth centuries.

But practically nothing of a saga literature survives. We move almost directly from heroic to romantic, from praise-poems about real men to invented stories about shadowy figures. The usual solution to this difficulty has been to ascribe a higher and older historical content to the romances. I would suggest that this need not necessarily be the case. The epic forms flourish best in relatively stable societies, whose traditions are relatively undisturbed. In Wales, at the precise moment when we might expect to find this form, with its often valuable historical framework, the Welsh-speaking areas were undergoing violent changes and contractions: the north British tribes were either cut off or came into Wales proper as outsiders, the links with Cornwall were growing weaker and its language more distinct. There was therefore what amounted to a conflict of material: looking back three generations, the picture of Britain as it had been was vastly different and difficult to grasp, while the north British traditions that had been 'imported' presented a version of the past which did not correspond to present realities, either geographically or in spirit.

The conundrum – for such it must have amounted to – was resolved by the bards by adopting a much freer attitude to fact, the outlook which characterizes the beginnings of romance. Taking names and places as a framework, they built their own stories out of such materials as were to hand. The often contradictory and overlapping traditions that resulted are the strongest evidence for this view, contradictions that were further multiplied by the 'antiquarian' period of the ninth century, when the revival of Welsh power in the kingdom of Gwynedd in north-west Wales and the beginnings of a written literature encouraged research into the past. The last layer of concealment is provided by the lateness of most of the Welsh manuscripts: the triads are found only in versions which lead back no further than the late twelfth century, and it is much more difficult to distinguish early and late material because of their highly abbreviated form. However, since the triads have traditionally been accorded an early place in Welsh tradition, as the key to lost sagas or romances, it is to them that we shall turn next.

The triads tend to confirm this view of Arthur as a later intruder. Thirteen of the surviving triads mention him, while another ten mention his court. A small part of the material is quite obviously from the period after the Latin and French romances, the mid-twelfth century onwards. Another group belong to the same milieu that produced the eleventh-century Welsh romances, where Arthur appears as centre of a glittering court of heroes from many places and periods. This leaves eight triads directly related to Arthurian tradition of the ninth century or earlier, two of which relate to his wife Gwenhwyfar.[9] The nature of the triads means that we gain no more than a glimpse of a story in some cases: one triad speaks of 'Three Men of the Island of Britain Qualified to Rule: Gwalchmei son of Gwyar, and Llacheu son of Arthur and Riwallawn Broom-hair'. As so often in the triads, the exact meaning of the epithet 'Qualified to Rule' is in doubt: its meaning ranges from wealthy to well-born: and other references in early poetry do not greatly help us. Such poetry as has survived from the tenth century and before is largely fragmentary, often exceedingly obscure, and defies classification. The fragments tell us the following about Llacheu:

> Cai the Fair and Llachau, they made slaughter . . .
> > *Dialogue with Glewlwyd Gavelvawr*[10] (see p. 69–71).

> I have been where was slain Llacheu, son of Arthur,
> Marvellous (?) in songs (or crafts), where ravens croaked
> > over blood.
> > *Stanzas of the Graves*[11] (see p. 67).

He occurs again in an artificial list of heroes in the romance *The Dream of Rhonabwy*, and occasionally in later poets. Beyond his standing as a warrior, however, nothing more emerges, except that some early tradition has been lost.* It is not even certain that Llacheu's father is the same as the two Arthurs we have already identified.

Two other triads which are at first sight early prove to depend on their meaning on other material. That in which Arthur appears as a swineherd, probably belongs to the same milieu as the descriptions of him in the lives of the Welsh saints written in the late eleventh and early twelfth centuries, as a kind of degenerate description of his role as boar hunter, though in view of the importance of the pig in Celtic culture, swineherd is not necessarily a degrading office; it may be that Arthur has displaced an earlier hero. That in which he is said to have disclosed 'the Head of Bran the Blessed from the White Hill, because it did not seem right to him that the Island should be defended by the strength of anyone, but by his own' is a pendant, as one of the 'Three Unfortunate Disclosures', to the 'Three Fortunate Concealments of the Island of Britain' (already a late item, with its reference to London), and belongs to the post-romance tradition. The story of Brân in this form is probably of the early twelfth century, and the addition of the disclosure seems a contrived literary device.

There remain a small group of triads which provide a glimmer of a definite story about Arthur. They read as follows:†

54   Three Unrestrained Ravagings of the Island of Britain:
    The first of them [occurred] when Medrawd came to Arthur's court at Celliwig in Cornwall; he left neither food nor drink in the court that he did not consume. And he dragged Gwenhwyfar from her royal chair and then he struck a blow upon her;

---

* Or misunderstood – *llecheu* means 'stones' and it would be tempting to 'explain away' Llacheu as a confusion from *Llecheu Arthur*, a landscape feature associated with Arthur, like Carn Cabal, the tenth of Nennius's *Mirabilia* (*see* p. 110).

† It is interesting to note that Aedan, father of the northern Arthur, appears in triad 54; and there is even a tradition that the battle of Arfderydd (triad 84) was fought between him and Rhydderch.

The second Unrestrained Ravaging [occurred] when Arthur came to Medrawd's court. He left neither food nor drink in the court;

(And the third Unrestrained Ravaging [occurred] when Aeddan the Wily came to the court of Rhydderch the Generous at Alclud [=Dumbarton]; he left neither food nor drink nor beast alive.)

53   Three Harmful Blows of the Island of Britain
The first of them Matholwch the Irishman struck upon Branwen daughter of Llyr;

The second Gwenhwyfach struck upon Gwenhwyfar: and for that cause there took place afterwards the Action of the Battle of Camlan;

And the third Golydan the Poet struck upon Cadwaladr the Blessed.

59   Three Unfortunate Counsels of the Island of Britain:
To give place for their horses' fore-feet on the land to Julius Caesar and the men of Rome, in requital for Meinlas;

and the second: to allow Horsa and Hengist and Rhonwen into this Island;

and the third: the three-fold dividing by Arthur of his men with Medrawd at Camlan.

84   Three Futile Battles of the Island of Britain:
One of them was the Battle of Goddeu: it was brought about by the cause of the bitch, together with the roebuck and the plover;

The second was the Action of Ar[f]derydd, which was brought about by the cause of the lark's nest;

And the third was the worst: that was Camlan, which was brought about because of a quarrel between Gwenhwyfar and Gwennhwy[f]ach.

This is why those [Battles] were called Futile: because they were brought about by such a barren cause as that.[12]

Even such a brief compass as this gives us two alternative versions of the story. Either because of Medrawd's assault on Gwenhwyfar, or because of a quarrel between Gwenhwyfach and Gwenhwyfar, Arthur fought Medrawd at Camlan with apparently disastrous results. It is possible that Gwenhwyfach is a 'shadow' of Gwenhwyfar, and that Medrawd's name should be substituted in two of the triads, particularly as Gwenhwyfach scarcely appears outside the triads. We would then have a fairly coherent tradition. But there is no reason to reject the two Arthurs we have already discussed as candidates for the central figure in this episode, unless we can clearly show that neither could possibly be associated with Medrawd, Gwenhwyfar or Camlan.

The evidence of the triads does not make Medrawd into the familiar treacherous figure of Mordred; he appears simply as a rival prince, perhaps husband of Gwenhwyfach. It would even be possible, if there were two blows 'struck upon Gwenhwyfar' (one by Gwenhwyfach, another, unrelated to Camlan, by Medrawd) to read triad 84 in such a way as to make Medrawd an ally of Arthur. Later Welsh sources add very little to our picture of him, except to portray him in conventional terms as brave and generous. The name is an uncommon one, found chiefly in Cornwall and Brittany. In the genealogies Medrawd only appears once, in a genealogy based on Geoffrey of Monmouth's *History of the Kings of Britain*, though he is also confused by one writer with Medrod son of Caradoc.[13] Gwenhwyfar is likewise a shadowy figure in early Welsh literature. She does not appear in the genealogies at all. Her name is an unusual one, and apparently connected with the Irish Finnabair. On this basis a claim could be made out for her as wife of either Arthur of Dyfed or Arthur of Dalriada, both of whom had Irish antecedents, and could have married a wife with an Irish name. Alternatively, the name may mean 'Gwenhwy the great' as opposed to her mysterious sister Gwenhwyfach (Gwenhwy the little): but the latter, as we have said, is quite probably an invented figure, a double of Gwenhwyfar.

One story does, however, survive about her, apart from passing references in the Welsh romances. It is from the same Latin *Life of St Gildas* that has already been quoted, which belongs to the antiquarian days of the early eleventh century, when the

Norman incursions had aroused new curiosity as to Welsh history, both on the part of the Normans and of the Welsh themselves. The author of the *Life of St Gildas*, Caradoc of Llancarfan, belonged to a sophisticated Normanized society, perhaps the abbey at Glastonbury, but he knew Welsh, and had access to traditional material. Gildas arrives at Glastonbury to find that it is under siege.

It was besieged by the ruler Arthur with a countless multitude because of Guennuvar his wife who had been violated and carried off by the aforesaid wicked king [i.e. Melvas, then 'reigning in the summer county'], bringing her there because it was an impenetrable place, defended by reeds, rivers and marsh. The rebellious king [i.e. Arthur]* had searched for the queen for a whole year, and had at last heard that she was there. At this news he raised the armies of all Cornwall and Devon, and the enemies prepared for war.

Seeing this, the abbot of Glastonbury and his clergy and Gildas the Wise went out between the battle lines and peaceably counselled Melvas his king to return the lady he had carried off. So she was returned, as she should have been, in peace and goodwill. This done, the two kings endowed the abbot with much territory; and they came to visit the temple of the Virgin Mary and to pray, the abbot confirming their blessed brotherhood ... So the Kings were reconciled and returned promising to obey in reverence the most reverend abbot of Glastonbury and never to violate that most holy place, or even the districts adjoining it.[14]

If Caradoc's framework is blatantly designed to the greater glory of Glastonbury, to the greater prestige of its abbot as chastiser of princes, and to the greater antiquity of its title to certain lands, the story which he has used to this end had an earlier existence independent of the Somerset foundation. We cannot even rely on the detail that Melvas was king of the summer county; this could be merely another local embellishment, though *Gwlad yr Haf* (i.e. the summer country) is the early Welsh name for Somerset. A fragment of a poem based

* An epithet which Caradoc uses in the passage about Arthur and Gildas quoted on p. 32..

5

on an episode in the story of Melvas and Guinevere survives in two relatively recent manuscripts: it is in a relatively primitive *englyn* form, and may be as old as the eleventh century.[15] It is very obscure, but appears to be a dialogue between Melvas and Gwenhwyfar, with perhaps a third speaker intervening, either Cai or Arthur. One of the speakers asks who the man sitting in the common part of the hall is, and Melvas identifies himself, saying he has had no wine. He is told that there is no wine for 'men who cannot hold out in the fray', and a dispute between him and Gwenhwyfar as to his strength compared with that of Cai begins, Gwenhwyfar vaunting Cai's prowess while Melvas boasts of his own. Gwenhwyfar says she has seen Melvas before in the court of Devon, and with more taunts and an exchange of blows, perhaps between Cai and Melvas, the fragment ends. It does not mention Arthur by name, though Cai's appearance in other poems links him closely with Arthur, and it is reasonable to assume that Arthur is the third speaker. The poem was probably inserted into a prose narrative, now lost, which would have been the original of Caradoc's story in the *Life of St Gildas*. Even so, these are both relatively late pieces, and there is a strong possibility that the story they contain belongs to those in which Arthur has replaced an earlier hero. It is possible that two separate stories, the rape of Gwenhwyfar and Arthur's battle with Medrawd have been merged due to similarity of the names Melvas and Medrawd, Gwenhwyfar becoming Arthur's wife in the process, in order to provide a reason for the battle of Camlan. Neither Medrawd, Gwenhwyfar nor Camlan has any particularly early place in the literary tradition and there is nothing to associate them with any definite period.

Apart from the triads, a number of early fragmentary pieces of poetry mention Arthur. Because they all appear in late manuscripts, it is difficult to date them, but they largely represent work of the tenth or eleventh century. In some cases, his name only is mentioned, but there are four more substantial pieces. The first from the Black Book of Carmarthen of about 1200 mentions him in connection with a battle fought by Gereint son of Erbin at a place called Llongborth: 'At Llongborth I saw belonging to Arthur bold men who hewed with steel; the emperor, the ruler in the toil of battle.'[16] Gereint is usually accepted as a king of Dumnonia (i.e. Devon); he appears in *The Gododdin* as 'Gereint from the south'. If the *Gododdin* evidence is to be relied upon, this would place him in the same milieu as Arthur of Dalriada; and an alliance between the two would fall naturally into place, either as part of Gereint's north British expedition, or as either prelude to or consequence of that expedition. The poet says nothing about Arthur's presence at the battle, though Arthur's men are clearly Gereint's allies. The only suspicious feature is the use of the word *amherwdyr* from the Latin *imperator*, which would suggest that the text has been influenced by Geoffrey of Monmouth's exaggerations. However, this may be a slight revision only, and the substance of the verse is probably earlier than Geoffrey.

Also in the Black Book of Carmarthen are the much debated verses known as the *Stanzas of the Graves*, recording the burial places of the heroes of the Welsh romances. They are perhaps as early as the tenth century, though exact dating is not possible. They may have served a similar purpose to the triads, inciting the audience to ask the bard to tell the stories of the heroes named; or they may be no more than an exercise in nostalgia, like Villon's 'Ballade des Dames du Temps Jadis':

> Dites moi où, n'en quel pays
> Est Flora la belle Romaine,
> Archipiades, ne Thaïs,
> Qui fut sa cousine germaine,
> Echo, parlant quant bruit ou maine,
> Dessus riviere ou sus estan,
> Qui beauté eut trop plus qu'humaine.
> Mais où sont les neiges d'antan?

Whichever interpretation we choose, the heroes named must have been famous in story or verse. But the entry for Arthur is altogether unusual:

> There is a grave for March, a grave for Gwythur,
> a grave for Gwgawn Red-sword;
> the world's wonder a grave for Arthur.[17]

The last line (*anoeth bit bet y arthur*) has been the subject of much debate. *Anoeth* has been variously translated as 'an eternal wonder' or 'unknown', though the general meaning is clear. *Anoeth* is an unusual word; its plural *anoetheu* is 'used several times in the prose tale of *Culhwch and Olwen* for the wonderful things which the hero has to find before he can win Olwen for wife. In combination with "*byd*" the word means "the wonder of the world" or "the most difficult thing in the world to find".'[18] Elsewhere in the *Stanzas of the Graves* there is a reference to 'the war-band of Oeth and Anoeth', buried at Gwanas, east of Dolgellau in Merioneth. Caer Oeth and Anoeth (the castle of Oeth and Anoeth) also appears in an addition to triad 52, 'Three Exalted Prisoners of the Island of Britain':

And one, who was more exalted than the three of them, was three nights in prison in Caer Oeth and Anoeth, and three nights imprisoned by Gwen Pendragon, and three nights in an enchanted prison under the Stone of Echymeint. This Exalted Prisoner was Arthur. And it was the same lad who released him from each of these three prisons – Goreu, son of Custennin, his cousin.[19]

Again, in the porter Glewlwyd's speech in *Culhwch and Olwen*, he remembers how he 'was of old in Caer Oeth and Anoeth'. On the face of it, an old tradition connected Arthur with this mysterious place, 'the castle of wonders and great wonders' or 'of difficulties and greater difficulties'. But it is also possible that the line in the *Stanzas of the Graves* inspired the connection, and that Oeth and Anoeth was an independent concept. The chronology and background of the various pieces would suggest that this was indeed the case. The speech in

Culhwch and Olwen is a fairly random collection of famous places from literature, and 'Oeth and Anoeth' could have been garnered from the *Stanzas of the Graves*; the triad seems to be later than the romance, and might perhaps have been invented in the light of Glewlwyd's speech. What lay behind the phrase was already forgotten by the time the author of *Culhwch* came to use it.

The other two Arthurian poems are more substantial. The first, again from the Black Book of Carmarthen, introduces Glewlwyd Gavaelvawr, the porter of Arthur's court in *Culhwch and Olwen*, apparently trying to shut out Arthur and his companion Cai. It is possible that the writer of *Culhwch*, a relatively late, 'literary' rather than oral work (*c.* 1080–1100), has given Arthur the most famous porter of whom he had heard, and that this poem represents the original tradition in which Glewlwyd was Arthur's foe. Alternatively, it may merely be a poetic device to make Arthur describe his feats. The poem (which is incomplete) runs as follows:

> What man is the gate-keeper?
> *Glewlwyd Mighty Grasp.*
> *What man asks it?*
> Arthur and fair Cai.
> *What [company] goes with you?*
> The best men in the world.
> *Into my house thou shalt not come*
> *unless thou warrant them* (?)
> I will warrant them
> and thou wilt see them.
> Wythneint, Elei, and Ssiwyon all three,*
> Mabon son of Mydron
> the servant of Uthyr Pendragon,
> and Gwyn Godyfrion.

* These could conceivably be adjectives – 'quick to anger, . . .: and wise all three'. Likewise *Tryfrwyd*, seven lines further on, could be an adjective meaning 'variegated, speckled with blood, pierced', but as the proper name occurs later in the poem this seems the less likely alternative.

My servants were fierce in defending their rights;
Manawydan son of Llyr
profound was his counsel.
Indeed Manawyd brought shattered shields from Tryfrwyd
And Mabon son of Mellt
he spotted the grass with blood;
and Anwas the Winged
and Llwch of the Striking Hand (?)
they were defending Eidyn on the border (?)
A lord would cherish them
to enhance his own appearance.*
Cai entreated them
as he hewed them down by threes.
When Celli was lost,† men endured cruelty.
Cai mocked them as he cut them down –
Arthur, though he was laughing (?).
the blood was flowing.
In the hall of Awarnach
fighting with a hag.
He smote the chief [or 'head'] of Palach
in the settlements of Dissethach,
on the mountain of Eidyn
he fought with the 'Dog-heads'.
They fell by the hundred,
by the hundred they fell
before Bedwyr Strong Sinew (?);
on the banks of Tryfrwyd
fighting with Garwlwyd.
Furious was his nature
with shield and sword.
A host was futile
compared with Cai in battle.
He was a blade in battle,
to his hand [hostages] were delivered.
They were steady leaders of an army
for the benefit of their country:
Bedwyr and Brydlaw.

* i.e. status?
† Cf. Celliwig, named as Arthur's capital in the triads and *Culhwch and Olwen*.

Nine hundred to listen
Six hundred [of them] to shout
who were fit for an attack.
I used to have servants —
it was better when they were alive.
Before the kings of Emrys*
I saw Cai hurrying.
He carried away booty
the 'long man'† was hostile (?).
Heavy was his vengeance,
fierce was his anger.
When he drank from a buffalo-horn
it was for four that he drank;
when he would come into battle
by the hundred he would slay.
Unless it were God who should cause it
the death of Cai were impossible.
Cai the fair and Llachau
they made slaughter.
Before the pang [i.e. 'death'?] from blue spears
on the heights of Ystafinion
Cai killed nine witches.
Cai the fair went to Môn
to destroy hosts [or 'lions'?].
His shield was a fragment (?)
Against Palug's Cat.
When people ask
'Who killed Palug's Cat?'
Nine score fierce [warriors] would fall as her food,
Nine score champions...[20]

Arthur's speech (like that of Glewlwyd in *Culhwch*, which might almost be a satire on the genre) brings in a vast mass of almost unknown episodes. The manner is again of a period when old traditions, half-forgotten already, were collected for their own sake, with little knowledge of what lay behind them. We can only unravel a few details. First, Cai reappears in an

* = Ambrosius in Nennius.
† i.e. Cai.

important role. His name has been derived from the Latin Caius; but he may also be of Irish origin: there is a legendary Irish figure named Cai Caínbrethach. He appears with Bedwyr as Arthur's companion in both the triads and the saints' lives, though we learn little more about him than the poem above tells us. He does not figure in the genealogies, and it has been suggested that his name 'Cei mab Kenyr' represents a 'doublet', Path son of Way, such as is found in the namelists in *Culhwch and Olwen* and elsewhere, which would account for his absence. It is curious that Bedwyr should also lack a true pedigree; he is called 'map Bedrawc', *pedrawc* meaning 'perfect', or, as in this poem, *bedrydant*, perhaps 'perfect of sinew'.[21] Both Cai and Bedwyr are conventional heroic figures, who have probably acquired adventures belonging to other forgotten characters; the list of Cai's exploits bristles with obscurities. Only Môn (Anglesey) and Palug's Cat, later associated with Arthur, are known from other sources. The overall impression is of a mythical monster-slaying hero, with little reality about him, and other sources are not more forthcoming about either him or Bedwyr, though the latter does appear in the *Stanzas of the Graves* in the same verse as a reference to Camlan:

> The grave of Osfran's son is at Camlan
> After many a slaughter;
> The grave of Bedwyr is on Tryfan hill.[22]

Of the other characters and episodes invoked, Gwyn Godyfrion, Manawydan son of Llyr, Anwas the Winged and Llwch Llawwynnawc appear in the list of warriors invoked by Culhwch in *Culhwch and Olwen*, while Mabon son of Modron appears elswhere in the same story. Furthermore, the last exploit of the story is the slaying of a hag by Arthur, and Awarnach the giant is also slain, for the sake of his sword. So the dialogue or the material to which it refers must have been known to the writer of the romance: but this offers us little help with its interpretation. Some of the same confusions are present: Mabon son of Modron and Mabon son of Mellt appear in both as separate persons, but the episodes in the hall of Awarnach and in the hag's cave have been combined. It would seem that both poem and romance belong to the same period of the recording of oral tradition, and are a warning as to the difficulties that occurred when bardic stories were written down: for instance, both writers have brought in characters with no Arthurian connections, such as the Celtic divine heroes Manawydan son of Llyr (originally the Irish sea-god Manannan mac Lir), Mabon map Modron (Maponus son of Matrona, a Celtic Apollo) and Llwch 'of the Striking Hand' (another Irish divinity). It is possible that Garwlwyd (Gwrgi Garwlwyt in the triads) may also be a mythical figure; the name seems to be 'Rough-grey man-hound' and suggests a werewolf, an idea supported by a parallel in Irish literature.[23]

However, Arthur's deeds may conceivably be part of an earlier tradition. Despite the contradictions, *Culhwch and Olwen* and the *Dialogue with Glewlwyd* both preserve a similar story, of a battle between Arthur and a hag somewhere in the north. In *Culhwch* the setting is purely formal:

Said Arthur, 'is there any of the marvels still unobtained?' Said one of the men, 'There is: the blood of the Black Witch, daughter of the White Witch, from the head of the Valley of Grief in the uplands of Hell.' Arthur set out for the North and came to where the hag's cave was.[24]

In the *Dialogue with Glewlwyd*, the setting is again the north, the borders near Eidyn; Eidyn is identifiable as Edinburgh on the evidence of *The Gododdin*.[25] Of Dissethach no trace remains as a place-name; but the head of Palach may be Palug's Cat (Cath Palug) under a different guise. Later tradition always represents Arthur as the slayer of the 'Chapalu', and the present poem may reflect the transfer of this exploit from Cai to Arthur.

This leaves only two names: the place Tryfrwyd and the person Uthr Pendragon. The manuscript reading in both cases is 'trywriud', which may be either a place-name or may mean 'variegated' (in colour or surface) as in another early poem.[26] The problem of Uthr Pendragon is a similar one: *uthr* is an adjective meaning 'terrible' or 'marvellous' as in the lines on Llacheu, Arthur's son: 'Llacheu, son of Arthur, marvellous in songs . . .' (Llacheu mab arthur uthir ig kerteu). Other references which clearly define Uther as a person are all later than Geoffrey of Monmouth's *History of the Kings of Britain*, and attempts to make him out as a character in Welsh tradition remain unconvincing.[27] The suggestion that Geoffrey misunderstood his source (i.e. the quotation given above) is much more probable, in which case the passage in the *Dialogue with Glewlwyd* would describe Mabon as 'the marvellous servant of Pendragon (i.e. the chief dragon)'. Mabon appears as just such a 'marvellous servant' in *Culhwch and Olwen*, while 'dragon' is often used of warriors in early poetry. The only other substantial evidence for Uther is a triad where he appears as the worker of an enchantment; likewise, in Geoffrey's story of Arthur's birth, Uther assumes the shape of Ygerna's husband in order to beget Arthur. Geoffrey has borrowed this theme from classical myth, endowing Uther with magical powers for the purposes of his plot. Hence the triad reference to Uther as enchanter could well derive from Geoffrey, if it does not arise from a play on the word *uthr*, marvel, in the *Dialogue with Glewlwyd*.

The substance of Arthurian tradition contained in the *Dialogue with Glewlwyd* is disappointingly slight: we learn little more than that Arthur was a great slayer of monsters, perhaps in the north, and that he had two companions of a similar bent, Bedwyr and Cai, Cai being as impressive a warrior as Arthur himself.

The last poem in the early Welsh tradition offers more sub-

stantial fare. *Preiddeu Annwfn* or *The Spoils of Annwfn* is as
cryptic as the *Dialogue with Glewlwyd*, but vastly more coherent
in outline.

> I worship the Lord, the Sovereign, the King of the Realm
> > [i.e. heaven],
> Who hath extended his sway over the world's strand.
> Perfect [i.e. richly equipped] was the prison of Gweir in the
> > Faery Fortress [Kaer Siddi],
> According to the tale of Pwyll and Pryderi.
> No one before him went into it,
> Into the heavy blue [i.e. steel] chain which held him, faithful
> > youth,
> And before the spoils of Annwn dolefully be chanted
> And till the Judgment he will remain in bardic song.
> > [*or*, our bardic prayer will last]
> Three shiploads of Prydwen we went into it;
> Save seven none returned from the Faery Fortress [Kaer Siddi].

> I am illustrious if song be heard. [*or*, ... illustrious, my song
> > was heard]
> In the Four-Cornered Fortress [Kaer Pedryvan], four-sided,
> My first utterance, it is from the caldron that it was spoken,
> By the breath of nine maidens it [i.e. the caldron] was kindled.
> Even the Chief of Annwn's caldron, what is its nature?
> Dark blue [i.e. enamel] and pearls are round its rim.
> It will not boil the food of a coward; it has not been destined.
> The sword of Llwch Lleawc was ... to it, [? sought from it]
> And in the hand of Lleminawc it was left.
> And before the gateway of hell lamps were burning,
> And when we went with Arthur, – glorious hardship, –
> Save seven none returned from the Fortress of Carousal
> > [Kaer Veddwit].

> I am illustrious! song is heard.
> In the Four Cornered Fortress [Kaer Pedryvan], the isle of the
> > active door, [*or*, the mighty defence of the island]
> Noonday and jet-blackness are mingled.
> Bright wine was their liquor before their retinue.
> Three shiploads of Prydwen we went on the sea;
> Save seven none returned from the Fortress of ... [Kaer Rigor].

I, lord of letters, do not reward mean folk. [*or*, do not deserve
                          (to deal with) mean men]
Beyond the Fortress of Glass [Kaer Wydyr] they saw not the
                          prowess of Arthur.
Three score hundred men stood on the wall.
It was difficult to converse with their sentinel.
Three shiploads of Prydwen went with Arthur;
Save seven none returned from the Fortress of . . .
                          [Kaer Goludd].[28]

Three further stanzas follow: two evidently refer to the same
expedition, ending in the same refrain as the previous ones, the
castles being Kaer Fandwy and Kaer Ochreu; and the last stanza
seems to be a mockery of the monks for their ignorance of
mythical lore. But all three are so difficult that no scholar has
yet offered a modern translation.

A vast amount of Welsh tradition has been compressed into
this short poem. The basic episode, a raid by Arthur to fetch a
magic cauldron, reappears in *Culhwch and Olwen*:

After that Arthur sent a messenger to Odgar son of Aedd king of
Ireland, to ask for the cauldron of Diwrnach the Irishman, his
overseer. Odgar besought him to give it. Said Diwrnach, 'God
knows, though he should be the better for getting one glimpse of
it, he should not have it.' And Arthur's messenger came back from
Ireland with a nay. Arthur set out and a light force with him, and
went in Prydwen his ship, and came to Ireland, and they made for
the house of Diwrnach the Irishman. The hosts of Odgar took note
of their strength; and after they had eaten and drunk their fill
Arthur demanded the cauldron. He made answer that were he to
give it to any one, he would have given it at the word of Odgar
king of Ireland. When he had spoken them nay, Bedwyr arose and
laid hold of the cauldron and put it on the back of Hygwydd,
Arthur's servant. His office was always to carry Arthur's cauldron
and to kindle fire under it. Llenlleawg the Irishman seized Caledfwlch
and swung it in a round and he slew Diwrnach the Irishman and all
his host. The hosts of Ireland came and fought with them. And
when the hosts were utterly routed Arthur and his men went on
board ship before their very eyes, and with them the cauldron full

of the treasures of Ireland. And they disembarked at the house of
Llwydeu son of Cel Coed, at Porth Cerddin in Dyfed.[29]

Preiddeu Annwfn is quite clearly the older of the two versions
of the story, deeply overlaid with mythical lore, to the extent
that it is a deliberate display of such knowledge. It is generally
accepted that the theme is that of an expedition to the Otherworld. Pwyll lord of Annwn appears with Pryderi his son in
the *Mabinogion* as lord of the Otherworld; the name Kaer Siddi
has similar connotations, and Kaer Pedryvan, Kaer Veddwit,
Kaer Rigor, Kaer Goludd and the other names are probably
epithets for the Otherworld as well. It is a specifically bardic
place: the themes of carousal and drinking evoke the atmosphere of feasts, and the cauldron is a cauldron of eloquence
from which the bards draw their inspiration. The opening lines
of each verse, and perhaps the last stanza, are also strongly
pagan in atmosphere. But there is a certain self-consciousness
about the writer's statements, almost a challenge to a rival
Christian culture which was beginning to usurp their old functions as historians and seers. This would place its composition
rather later than the lore which it uses, perhaps into the tenth
century: and, more important, it would be a conscious gathering of tradition rather than a single coherent legend. The poem
is preserved with similar pieces in the *Book of Taliesin*, and may
be a verse interlude from a prose tale about the poet; it is the
earliest link between Taliesin and Arthur.[30]

The story in stanza 4 reappears in Nennius's *History of the
Britons*, in a variant version, as part of the story of the occupation of Ireland.

Most recently, however, the Irish came from Spain to Ireland. Firstly
there came Partholomus with a thousand men and women and they
increased in Ireland to four thousand; and a sickness came upon
them and in one week they all perished and not a single one was left.
Secondly there came to Ireland Nimeth son of a certain Agnomen,
who sailed the seas for a year and a half and after that landed in

Ireland, his ships being wrecked. He remained there for many years; then sailing away with his men, he returned to Spain. And after that there came three sons of a Spanish knight with thirty ships and thirty couples in each ship and remained there for a year. Then they saw a glass tower in the middle of the sea, and men on the tower; and they tried to speak to them and they never replied. With one accord, they hastened to besiege the tower with all their ships and all their women, except for one ship which had been wrecked and its crew of thirty men and women aboard. The other ships sailed to besiege the tower, and while they were disembarking on the shore around the tower, the sea overwhelmed them and they were all drowned, not one escaping. And the whole of Ireland was populated from the men and women of the one damaged ship left behind down to the present day.[31]

Nennius has rationalized his version, but the tower of glass stands out as a borrowing from a patently poetic source. However, the strands may come together in a surprisingly rational way. Ynys Wair is an old name for Lundy, and this sheer-sided rock may be both 'the prison of Gwair' and Nennius's 'glass tower'. It would indeed be difficult to converse with a sentinel there; and furthermore, with Grassholm and Bardsey, it was traditionally regarded as a kind of Otherworld. It would be tempting to go further: to identify Nennius's Nimeth with Nimet of the genealogy of Arthur of Dyfed, and regard the episode as a memory of an expedition by one of Arthur's forebears from South Wales against Lundy. Some such exploit, though not necessarily connected with Arthur, may have been combined with half-forgotten pagan lore describing a mythical hero's expedition to the underworld; and the localization of the exploit at Lundy would naturally suggest Arthur of Dyfed with his South Welsh connections as a suitable leader. Mingled with this may be distant memories of expeditions to the Scottish islands, such as Aedan mac Gabrain's raid on the Orkneys in 580 or 581. The only other detail which suggests a deeper Arthurian connection is the presence of

Llwch of the Striking Hand (corruptly described as Lluch Lleawg or Lleminawg), who is also coupled with Arthur in the Black Book poem.

The diversity and obscurity of the Welsh material on Arthur make it difficult to generalize about his various appearances. He is personally brave and a leader of men: he never takes a subordinate part, and he never abandons the arts of war for more peaceful pursuits. A small group of figures are associated exclusively with him: Medrawd, Gwenhwyfar, Cai and Bedwyr. They have only the most shadowy characters: Cai and Bedwyr are warriors, Gwenhwyfar his wife, Medrawd perhaps his enemy. Beyond this group, Arthur's name is found in connection with a much older group of recognizably mythical figures, the shadows of pagan gods; but he always appears as an intruder, either gathering stray names around him to provide a following, or, as in *Preiddeu Annwfn*, as an aggressor against them. In the genealogies he is again unknown or inserted at a later date, except in the case of the house of Dyfed. We have made little progress from the unknown hero of the *Gododdin* line, 'although he was no Arthur'. The only certainty is Arthur's heroic standing; otherwise he is rootless, scarcely remembered by the early poets. He does not belong either to the primeval world of Celtic myth or to the great heroes of the poetic tradition; he is an outsider.

6 A Political Hero

The literature of tenth-century Wales belongs to a tradition fostered in a single milieu, that of the bards and *cyfarwyddiaid* or storytellers. But that tradition contains many different gleanings from history, genealogy, etymology, folktales and primitive religion. By contrast, the historical writing of the same period lacks the coherent tradition and is a very much more individual affair. Its basic material is simple in the extreme: bare chronicles of years and events such as those of the end of the Roman empire and of the Irish monasteries. Gildas's highly personal work stands alone; for many decades there was no incentive to attempt historical works in Latin on any scale.

The lack of a clear sense of the past is common to the whole of Europe during the seventh and eighth century. Only in peace could men survey the years gone by with a larger vision; under the stress of war, the present was all too demanding. The history of Wales in this period is a deep confusion of civil wars, Saxon defeats and separation from almost all contact with the outside world. The temporary victory of Cadwallawn over the Saxon Edwin in 633 and the equally shortlived triumph of the British alliance with Penda of Mercia are the two highlights which relieve the sombre years; and the defeat of Penda at Winwaed Field in 655 marked the end of British hopes of regaining territory outside the boundaries of modern Wales. In 664 the Synod of Whitby wooed the Northumbrian church away from its Celtic allegiance, and by 705, with the loss of Devon and Cornwall to the Roman cause, the Welsh alone remained outside its wider horizons and international contacts.

The following century was one of stagnation and the gradual relaxation of the warfare with the Saxons. The erection of Offa's Dyke as the Anglo-Welsh boundary in the latter part of the eighth century set the seal on Welsh isolation. Within the new, narrower confines of their territory, the principalities of medieval Wales gradually emerged. But the process was slow, and until the very end of the independent history of Wales, petty kings were always prone to carve out private territory of their own. The organization of Welsh society was such that the tribal distinctions and bonds of kinship remained strong; hence a kingdom was a conglomeration of small groups owing their first loyalty to the smaller unit rather than the larger. A problem familiar throughout Western Europe, it was at its most acute in Wales, and during the seventh and eighth centuries it is often impossible to draw a clear political picture of the country.

The contraction of Welsh territory and the shifting nature of its political structure played havoc with such historical records as existed. The historical memory of the people was centred on the bards; written chronicles have not survived, though it is possible that documents similar to the Irish annals were kept in the greater monasteries such as Bangor. The bards were closely allied to the royal house which they served; its over- throw would mean at worst the loss of their records and tradi- tions, at best their incorporation into those of the conqueror's family. In the case of the Britons of Strathclyde and Cumbria, it was only where their princes found new territories within Wales that their family histories were preserved. Poetry, al- though originally specific, was more adaptable: thus Taliesin's and Aneirin's works were revered as relics of a general heroic past and accepted by Welsh bards as such, although their subject matter was largely northern.

In this fluid and forcibly introverted society, cut off from outside contact by the Saxons and by the quarrel with the Roman church, the bards were to some extent deprived of their earlier material, the celebration of military glory. Their work grew increasingly allusive, a series of comparisons with the heroes of the past, and they drew on myths to extend their range. The *Laws of Hywel Dda* give the *penkerdd*, the chief bard, the duty of singing of 'one song to God and one song to the

6

king'; these would appear to be the traditional eulogies in the authentic bardic tradition. Besides these august figures, probably only to be found in the great courts, are the bards of the prince's retinue, who are allowed to use free metre, and probably to recite sagas; cast in a more popular mould, they were not so far from the ordinary storytellers who provided much of the entertainment of the common folk almost until the present century.

The sagas seem to belong to a later age than the elegiacs of the first known Welsh poetry. Yet they employ the characters of the early poetry, most notably in the poems attributed to Llywarch the Old. They are conscious inventions, and so open to all kinds of outside influence, which may explain why so much material extraneous to the original sagas, either from Irish sources or from native folklore, was accepted into Welsh poetry by the ninth and tenth centuries, if not before. Hence the historical value of the poetic tradition had been disturbed to a considerable degree by the beginning of the ninth century, partly by the instability of Welsh society, partly by the changing of poetic fashion, though the latter process was far from complete.

The early years of the ninth century saw the breaking down of Welsh isolation and introversion. The most important event in this process was a change of dynasty in Gwynedd, the chief of the Welsh kingdoms. It had been ruled throughout the preceding two centuries by the descendants of Maelgwn (Maglocunus) whom Gildas had castigated, and had retained its original territory and prestige despite a series of indifferent rulers. The man who ascended the throne in 825, Merfyn Vrych, was cast in a different mould. Though his mother was sister to the previous king, he himself seems to have been, if not an adventurer, certainly a man ready to seize an opportunity. Traditionally he came from the north of Britain (or possibly the Isle of Man) and was a descendant of Llywarch the Old. By an alliance with the rulers of Powys and by able government, he held Gwynedd securely for nineteen years, leaving it to his son Rhodri the Great. Rhodri imposed a unity on Wales such as it had not known since Roman days: only the kingdom of Dyfed and three other small states in the south were independent of his sway.

With the return of stability in Europe under the Carolingians, the intellectual traffic between Ireland and the continent, never totally extinguished, flourished as never before. The great school at Bangor on the Dee, already famous in the early seventh century, now served as staging post for wandering Irish monks *en route* for England or France. Though its monks lived 'by the labour of their hands', it was here that St Columbanus learnt lighthearted Latin verse in the seventh century, and its antiphonary contained Greek words when Greek was almost entirely forgotten elsewhere. With the new contacts of the late eighth and early ninth century, the vision of the world widened considerably. In 768, the Celtic church at long last accepted the Roman system of dating Easter at the instigation of 'that man of God, Elbodugus'. Elbodugus rose to become archbishop of Gwynedd, dying in 809, and his pro-Roman views must have smoothed the way for communications with the rest of the Church. Under Merfyn we find Irish scholars writing to their teacher Colgu at Merfyn's court about a cryptogram set by a visiting Irishman at Merfyn's court. The cryptogram involves a Latin sentence 'Mermin rex Conchen salutem' written in Greek letters; and the correspondence implies a steady stream of Irish scholars through Gwynedd.[1] The names of the scholars allow possible identification with known ecclesiastical figures on the continent; and Dubthach, who set the problem, might be the 'Dubthach mac Máel-Tuile, most learned of the Latin scholars of all Europe, who went to sleep in Christ in 868'. Even more interesting is a possible link with Sedulius Scottus, the greatest poet of the age, a considerable scholar and wit, who settled at Liège about 848, though this belongs to the age of Rhodri Mawr two or three decades later. Among Sedulius's poems is a short poem on the erection of an altar:[2]

> At this altar the glory of the saints prevails
> Enclosing the holy treasures of their relics;
> Here reigns a fragment of the precious cross of Christ
> Which conquered Hell and spread the heavenly kingdom's rule;
> His mother Mary's worship gilds this place,
> She, the Virgin, holding sway in high-throned paradise.
> This altar for all ages serves the apostles' glory
> Triumphant among them Peter and Paul in splendour.
> The ashes of the blessed martyrs sweeten the air,
> Among them Stephen, winner of that earliest crown.
> In king Rhodri's time, when Ratbald was chief priest,
> This sacred altar was ordained and made;
> And piously he's vowed to you, Lord Christ,
> And to the saints, offering to honour you all.

If we are right in identifying Roricus with Rhodri, despite the presence of the Germanic Ratbald, this is important evidence for Gwynedd's cultural links with the Continent. The altar in question might perhaps be at a shrine abroad, which would make both Sedulius's interest and Ratbald's presence more explicable. It was about the same time (854) that Concenn, ruler of Powys (connected with Merfyn in the cryptogram) died at Rome on pilgrimage, which again points to a widening of horizons.

So, for the first time in two centuries, the Welsh looked outward rather than inward. They became aware once again, with the weakening of Mercian power, of the possibilities of reconquest. Despite the new threats from Wessex in the south and from the Norsemen round their coasts, the immediate enemy across Offa's Dyke no longer seemed so formidable. At the same time, the new dynasty in Gwynedd were anxious to justify their title to the throne; and the result was a new interest in the old records and traditions of the bards. The inquirers were no longer the bards themselves, but men trained in the monkish learning. The style of the bards, grown obscure and introverted over the years, was both confusing to them and inadequate for their purpose. Even the genealogies were too spare in outline for them; everything needed to be reinterpreted and presented in their own language and mode of thought, a mode which was no longer exclusively religious. Gildas and his predecessors were using history for religious ends, as we have seen; the events of their own day were the result of the moral actions of past generations and were to some extent explained in terms of divine reward and punishment. But Gildas is also the precursor of writers such as Paul the Deacon and Gregory of Tours, in that his book is nationalist in scope. His scope is the British people, and particularly the British people as heirs of Rome. The same approach is found in both Paul the Deacon's *History of the Lombards* and Gregory of Tours's *History of the Franks* of the sixth and seventh centuries (Cassiodorus's *History of the Goths* survives only in later versions); Widukind of Corvey's *Deeds of the Saxons* and Saxo Grammaticus's *Deeds of the Danes* are later examples of the national history.

It is with these works that the earliest secular Latin work on Welsh history to have survived, Nennius's *History of the Britons*, must be classified. Nennius, writing in the early years of the ninth century, is both an antiquarian with political motives and an author conscious of continental traditions. We know very little about him personally. His name is akin to the Irish Ninian, but in a purely Welsh form.[3] In the preface found in some manuscripts, he describes himself as 'disciple of Elvodugus',[4] that is, the Elbodugus who had been responsible for the religious reform of 768. He was almost certainly a monk or at least a cleric, and it is possible that he was involved with the business of the royal courts of Wales as an interpreter. The evidence for this is slight but interesting. In a twelfth-century manuscript at Oxford, a curious alphabet is recorded, which, according to the accompanying text, was invented by a certain Nemnivus in argument with a Saxon scholar who denied the existence of a British alphabet, in order to 'refute the accusations of stupidity made against his people'. This phrase recurs in the preface to the *History of the Britons* (already mentioned): 'I, Nennius, the disciple of Elvodugus, have taken the trouble of writing down a few fragments which refute the stupidity of the British race . . .'[5] The amusing twist is that the alphabet given is clearly based on the Anglo-Saxon one; and elsewhere in the *History of the Britons* Nennius displays a knowledge of Anglo-Saxon and an interest in philology as well. When Vortigern attempted to make peace with Hengist both sides

. . . summoned a conference, so that Britons and Saxons could come together unarmed and seal their friendship. And Hengist ordered all his relatives to put their daggers beneath their feet inside their shoes. 'And when I shout to you: "*Eu Saxones eniminit saxas*," take out your knives from your shoes and hurl yourselves upon them and attack them fiercely.'[6]

The phrase in Saxon which Nennius gives (and which he immediately translates for the benefit of his audience) is probably an authentic tradition, as the words are not in the Anglo-Saxon of Nennius's day but in an earlier form.[7] Furthermore, Nennius emphasized that a knowledge of Saxon was unusual among the Welsh.

. . . Hengist gave a feast for Vortigern and his men and his interpreter, called Ceretic, and no other Briton among the Britons knew Saxon except this man; and he applied himself to acquiring a knowledge of it [*or* to reading it] until he was able to understand the Saxon speech.

If we take the second possible meaning of *legat*, 'he reads', this sounds like a piece of autobiography. In the words of one scholar, 'the rarity and importance of a Briton understanding English are so remarkably emphasized by Nennius that I cannot but suspect that he himself held the post of official interpreter at his prince's court near the English frontier'.[8] On the other hand, Bede, though he describes the five languages of the Island of Britain as English, British, Irish, Pictish and Latin, only mentions a translator during the episode of the conversion of the Pictish church to the Roman observance of Easter,[9] which would imply that they were common enough between Welsh and Saxons not to be noteworthy. Interpreters such as Bledri of Carmarthen were to play an important part in the development of the Arthurian legend in the twelfth century,[10] and it would be no surprise to find Nennius among their number.

We can supply a few further details about its author from the *History of the Britons* itself. Nennius used a fairly large range of Latin sources; one version of the preface lists 'the Roman annals, the writing of the Fathers of the Church, namely, Isidore, Jerome, Prosper and Eusebius', but there were others besides these relatively standard works. He also had before him an early German work, a mythical genealogy showing the Roman descent of the Franks; only one manuscript survives of the version which he used, now at Reichenau, which suggests that this may have reached him by way of Irish scholars; likewise, the *Life of St Germanus*, in whatever form he may have used it, was also of continental origin. Prosper Tiro's chronicle, written in Aquitaine, *c.* 420–60, wrongly classed on the preface as the work of a Father of the Church, is also a relatively uncommon work, and reinforces the idea of some contact with scholarly circles in France, as does his use of the *Epitome* of Aurelius Victor.[11] His quotation of Virgil in chapter 20 is taken from Eusebius's narrative, so that these four works are the only manuscripts which are in any way out of the ordinary. Isidore, Jerome and Eusebius would have been part of the ordinary library of any major monastic foundation, even in the relative isolation of Wales. The British sources which he employed are part of a different problem; the list above gives us a reasonably clear idea of his contact with classical and European culture.

The next and most vexed question of all is that of the exact date and composition of the *History of the Britons*; it has been said 'that no problem of the early Middle Ages presents greater difficulties than the origin and textual history of the compilation of the *Historia*'.[12] The detailed arguments are beyond the scope of the present book; all that can be offered here is an outline of the main possibilities. None of the surviving manuscripts is earlier than AD 900, and, ironically, the two earliest of these are generally accepted as being edited, or at least badly transcribed versions. One, the manuscript at Chartres, breaks off in the middle of chapter 36 (the episode of Hengist's treachery): and although it is the oldest extant version, it is so much at variance with the other manuscripts that it will not be of much help for our purpose. The other early version, in the Vatican and in a later MS at Paris, is headed 'Here begins the history of the Britons written by (*edita*) the hermit Mark, a holy bishop of the said race'. But this has additions and comments which make it plain that it is later than the version of the text contained in twelfth-century manuscripts. The basic text is therefore the British Museum manuscript, Harleian 3859, dated to the late eleventh or early twelfth century. It contains other Welsh material, the *Annals of Wales* and the genealogies already discussed, and was evidently a deliberate collection of material on Welsh history. It is bound with two other unrelated manuscripts, and nothing certain is known of its history before it came into the collection of Robert Harley in the early eighteenth century.[13]

The remaining manuscripts are all of the twelfth or thirteenth century. They fall into different groups, according to their preface; which poses our first major problem. The preface varies to the extent of attributing the work to either Gildas or

Nennius, or leaving it anonymous. The Harleian manuscript and one other closely related to it omit the preface altogether; three twelfth- and thirteenth-century manuscripts attribute the book to Gildas; and two twelfth-century copies (as well as the Irish version of Gilla mac Coemain) give Nennius as author. Gildas is unquestionably not the author, though large passages depend on his work; but as he was an almost legendary figure, either comparison with the *De Excidio* or his name alone may have suggested the attribution. Furthermore, the Durham manuscript mentions both Gildas and Nennius, though the attribution to the latter would seem to be the result of comparison with another manuscript. However, a solution to the problem of these variations is not impossible. The loss of an initial leaf from the Harleian manuscript or one of its predecessors would be a sufficient explanation; but it also seems likely that the present version is not Nennius's original work. The evidence as to the date of composition in particular would indicate a series of different editions (perhaps keeping pace with the requirements of the court of Gwynedd), of which there are traces of at least three, apart from the Chartres and Vatican versions. In the course of this editing at least one of Nennius's successors omitted the prologue as part of his alterations, retaining the Saxon genealogies which are omitted in the versions which include the preface. This omission is explained by the scribe, in a note at the end, on the grounds that his master Beulan had already studied them and pronounced them useless (probably because of the presence of Woden at the beginning of each genealogy).

The problem of dating the original version of the *History of the Britons* is excessively difficult. The internal evidence in the Harleian version is as follows: the last and presumably contemporary Saxon king mentioned is Ecgfrith of Mercia (who reigned for a few months in 796); there is a reference to Fernmail as ruler of 'Buelt et Guorthigerniaun' in east Wales (who perhaps reigned *c*. 800); and in a chronological calculation in chapter 16 there is a reference to Merfyn Vrych as being in the fourth year of his reign. The first two pieces of evidence are by no means certain indicators. The reference to Ecgfrith appears in a collection of Saxon genealogies; these form a self-contained section, and are generally agreed to be copied from a Saxon manuscript. (This argument would also reinforce Nennius's claim to authorship, in view of his knowledge of Saxon.) All that the appearance of Ecgfrith proves is that Nennius's original was written in 796; it tells us nothing about the date at which it was included in the *History of the Britons*. The allusion to Fernmail is equally open to various interpretations: all we know of him is that according to later tradition (in the genealogies) his cousin married Arthfail of Morgannwg. This need not necessarily be incompatible, in the absence of other evidence, with the clear date of 829, the fourth year of Merfyn Vrych,[14] mentioned as the date of composition elsewhere. His name once again appears as part of a genealogy, introduced with the words, 'This is their genealogy, traced back to the beginning. Fernmail is he who now reigns in the two regions of Buelt and Guorthigern, son of Teudubir. Teudubir was king of the region of Buelt, son of Pascent, son of Guoidcant . . . '[15] This passage is open to the same interpretation as the Saxon genealogies, that it has been copied without alteration from an earlier manuscript. In this case, the only valid date would be that of 829, which would not conflict with Nennius's description of himself as 'disciple of Elvodugus', since he could easily have survived the latter by twenty years.

Whatever the date of the present version, its value depends almost entirely on the sources on which Nennius drew, and his attitude towards them. The preface (with the repeated proviso that it may be a later invention) gives us some clues as to his problems; indeed, its ring of truth is one reason why it is difficult to reject it as a forgery:

I, Nennius, disciple of Elvodugus, have taken the trouble of writing down a few fragments which refute the stupidity of the British race [a charge brought against them], because their learned men had no knowledge and had not written in books any record of that island of Britain. But I have heaped together all that I could find, both in Roman annals and in the chronicles of the Fathers of the Church, that is Jerome, Eusebius, Isidore and Prosper, and also the annals of the Irish and Saxons and from the tradition of our elders. Which many learned men and men of books have tried to write, and which they abandoned as too difficult for I know not what reason; whether because of frequent deaths or the repeated ravages of wars. I ask that any reader who shall read this book shall pardon me for daring to write all this like a talkative bird or like some unworthy judge. I yield to him who will know more of this matter than I.[16]

The passages drawn from the classical authors whom he cites are of no especial value; the originals are well known, and he has no details to add. 'The annals of the Irish [Scottorum] and Saxons and . . . the tradition of our elders' are the important element, with one additional item not listed in the preface, the genealogy of the peoples of Europe. This last item is perhaps the most revealing. Nennius is the first writer to think of the Britons as having a 'history'. Where Gildas saw them as the inept heirs of Rome, Nennius portrays them as a race with as noble a pedigree as the Romans. Taking the Frankish story as his basis, he adapts it to include the Britons. The original gives Japhet's relation Alanus as the founder of Europe: 'The said Alanus had three sons, Hisisione, Ermenone and Nigueo. Four races sprang from Hisisione, the Romans, Franks, Germans and Britons . . .'.[17] With this clue, Nennius proceeds to invent an equivalent British genealogy (just as he had invented a British alphabet when national pride required it). Having filled in the details of Alanus's descent, he declares, 'This knowledge I found in the traditions of our elders who were the first inhabitants of this island',[18] and then describes the descent of Britto from Alanus, Britto giving his name to the Britons. However, he has already incorporated Britto into a genealogy which makes him of Roman descent, and proceeds, clumsily, to try to reconcile the two, producing yet another version as he does so. This episode gives us some clue as to what he meant by 'the traditions of our elders'; these were not necessarily oral, but included manuscripts such as the German genealogy. On the other hand, he does not respect them as much as he does the other works he cites, and is not above rewriting them extensively to suit his own views. The first adaptation, of the Roman genealogy, seems to be an emulation of Fredegar's eighth-century chronicle, giving the Franks a Trojan origin; faced with the second piece of evidence, Nennius has adapted it rather than reject it entirely.

The early part of the *History* contains some passages from unknown sources of great interest, such as the episode of the glass tower quoted earlier; but it is only when the information in Prosper Tiro's chronicle runs out that Nennius becomes our only source for the majority of the events he describes and really claims our attention. His narrative becomes largely independent from the beginning of chapter 31, describing the Saxon invasions, though he draws on the *Life of St Germanus* in the following chapter, and takes up an occasional hint from Gildas. The next eighteen chapters are concerned with the history of Vortigern and his relations with Hengist and Horsa. Bede's history of the Saxons has been suggested as a possible source, but a lost 'chronicle of the Saxons' would be more likely as the original of both narratives. Nennius's attitude to Vortigern, however, is coloured by political considerations. Vortigern's character first appears in Gildas, as the *superbus tyrannus*, the 'proud ruler' who had invited the Saxons to England; but in Nennius he also appears as an opponent of St Germanus and the discipline of the Roman Church. As a result, Nennius has erased his name from the genealogy of the kings of Powys, giving them instead a mysterious Catell Durnluc, subject of one of St Germanus's miracles, and therefore entirely orthodox, as ancestor. Vortigern does appear in the genealogy of Fernmail of Built, probably because this was copied in its entirety from another source.

Behind the story of Vortigern there may be traces of a genuine popular saga about him. But he does not appear in any of the early panegyric poetry, and it is not entirely easy to accept that such a saga existed in the absence of the survival of anything remotely parallel in form.[19] The hints in Gildas, the *Life of St Germanus* and the *Stanzas of the Graves* could have been sufficient to fire Nennius's imagination, especially as the episode of the boy Ambrosius seems to be adapted from an independent Welsh tale, and Vortigern's sins are of a fairly conventional type; similar stories occur both in Gregory of Tours's *History of the Franks* and in the Lombard histories, and are a stock monastic explanation for the failings of kings well into the Middle Ages.

The story of Vortigern is followed by a series of relatively disjointed pieces: Fernmail's genealogy, the life of St Patrick, the battles of Arthur, the Saxon genealogies, notes on north British and Saxon history, a list of the cities of Britain and another of the marvels of Britain. At this point we think of Nennius's remark in the preface: 'I have heaped together all I could find.' If his chronology and sense of sequence have been weak enough up to this point, he now abandons all pretence at relating his various discoveries to each other. Modern editors have suggested all kinds of changes of sequence to give a semblance of unity to the *Historia*; a better approach would be to simply bear in mind Nennius's own avowed method, which is to link quite unrelated passages with a vague 'in those days': no less than four sections of the *History* (chapters 32, 50, 56, 62) introducing new topics begin with these words, and similar phrases recur within the chapters without more precise meaning. This question of the structure and linking phrases is particularly important in chapter 56, the famous passage on

Arthur, which, now that we have examined the general background of the *History of the Britons*, we may quote in full:

In those days the Saxons increased in numbers and grew stronger in Britain. But at Hengist's death, Octha his son went from the northern part of Britain to the kingdom of Kent and from him arose the kings of Kent.

Then Arthur fought against those men in those days with the kings of the Britons, but he was leader of battles. The first battle was in the mouth of the river which is called Glein. The second and third and fourth and fifth on another river which is called Dubglas and is in the region Linnuis. The sixth battle on the river which is called Bassas. The seventh battle was in the forest of Celidon, that is Cat Coit Celidon. The eighth battle was at the fort of Guinnion, in which Arthur carried the image of the blessed Mary, ever-virgin, on his shoulders and the pagans were put to flight and there was a great slaughter of them by the grace of our Lord Jesus Christ and by the grace of blessed Mary the Virgin, his mother. The ninth battle was fought in the city of the Legion. He fought the tenth battle on the shore of the river called Tribruit. The eleventh battle was fought on the mountain called Agned. The twelfth battle was at Badon Hill, where nine hundred and sixty men perished at one charge of Arthur's and no-one killed them save he himself. And in all the battles he was victor. And they, when they were defeated in all the battles, sent for help to Germany, and their numbers were ceaselessly added to, and they brought kings from Germany to rule over those in Britain, until the time when Ida ruled, who was son of Eobba: he was the first king in Bernicia.[20]

The first question to be resolved is the placing of this passage in Nennius's somewhat vague chronology. At once we meet a difficulty: the text, as we have indicated, is at this point a miscellaneous collection, in no particular sequence. For example, the last phrase of the passage quoted leads into the so-called Northern History, the story of the struggle of the north British princes against the Saxons; but the phrase 'he was first king in Bernicia' has prompted the inclusion of the genealogies of the

Anglo-Saxon kings, which begin with the kings of Bernicia. The 'northern history' section seems to have been taken by Nennius from a collection of notes on the subject put together in the late eighth century, based largely on traditional material. While the chronology of events in the north British sequence is coherent, the attempts to relate them to the history of Wales are unreliable. For instance, Maelgwn of Gwynedd (died *c.* 547) appears after Aneirin, who is generally placed towards the end of the sixth century. Important events such as Edwin's death at Hatfield in 633 are omitted completely; and the impression left is of a relatively local and spasmodic record which has been woven into the more general scope of the *History of the Britons* by occasional attempts to relate it to events outside the range of the original writer.

Returning to the beginning of chapter 56, there is evidence of a similar process of the weaving in of additional material. In this case, the process has worked in reverse. The resistance of the Britons to Hengist and Horsa and their sons is originally told in chapter 43, as follows:

Meanwhile Guorthemir, son of Guorthigirn [Vortigern], fought obstinately with Hengist and Horsa and their people, and drove them back as far as the aforesaid island called Thanet, and three times shut them up there, besieged them, struck them down and terrified them. And they sent envoys across the sea to Germany, summoning ships with a huge number of men. And thereafter they fought with the kings of our people; sometimes they were victorious and expanded their boundaries; sometimes they were defeated and driven back. And Guorthemir eagerly fought four battles against them: the first battle was on the river Derguentid; the second on the ford called in their language Episford, but in our tongue Rithergabail, and there he killed Horsa and a son of Guorthigirn called Categirn; the third battle was in the plain near the inscribed stone on the shore of the Channel and the barbarians were defeated and he was the victor; they fled to their ships and were drowned as, fleeing like women, they tried to get into them. But he himself died a short while afterwards.[21]

The outline of this story – a British campaign against the Saxons, and the growth of the Saxons by reinforcement from Germany – is also that of chapter 56. The sentence about Octha derives from a narrative of the establishment of the Saxon kingdoms, beginning with that of Kent, which may have been no more than a simple list, giving the founder of each kingdom – Octha in Kent, Ida in Bernicia. It is an attempt to connect otherwise isolated material on north British resistance to the Saxons with Octha's campaign in the north, described in chapter 38. This was specifically against the Scotti, that is the Irish, around the Firth of Forth and one of the Roman walls – 'the wall which is called *Guaul*' is simply a tautology, *Guaul* being a Saxon corruption of the Roman *vallum*. Hence Arthur's exploits belong correctly to the north, the Kentish reference being a false trail. This is borne out by the continuation of the story not with affairs in Kent, but in Bernicia. Furthermore, recent editors have altered the old chapter division: such manuscripts as I have examined, including that generally regarded as the most reliable, clearly show a chapter initial (or a space for one) at the word *Tunc* ('Then Arthur . . .'). The linking nature of the passage about Octha is therefore quite clear in the text. Nor is the time correlation with Octha correct; Nennius has simply supplied the name of the only Saxon chief whom he can find who was supposed to have fought against the northern Scotti of the kingdom of Dalriada. The next sentence, which seems to pose all kinds of problems if we regard Arthur as a native Briton, now becomes clear. The 'Kings of the Britons' are being led by an Irish-British chieftain; hence the note '*but* he himself was leader of battles'. The later attempt in the variant Vatican manuscript to explain this by a note that 'although many were more noble than he, he was the leader and victor in twelve battles' arises out of the failure of Nennius (or his original) to include the reason why it was unlikely that he should have been the leader. The distinction between the 'Irish-

Britons' of Dalriada and the 'Welsh-Britons' of north-east
Scotland, originally not very great, had increased with the
isolation of Dalriada after the Saxon conquest of southern
Scotland. So it seems likely that Nennius's original contained
the information that Arthur came from Dalriada. Nennius,
wishing to include Arthur as a British hero, yet not daring to
actually contradict his source, discreetly omits this detail, only
to hint at it by his patriotic surprise at a prince of Dalriada
leading the British kings.

The list of battles that follows has provoked more com-
mentary than any other passage of early British history. For
each site there are a dozen proposed identifications, a dozen
possible theories. Arthur is envisaged as a soldier with Roman
or even Byzantine training, in charge of a fully equipped
cavalry force,[22] despite the relatively humble status of cavalry
in the armies of both empires, and the total lack of any supporting archaeological evidence for this period in Britain: no bridles,
bits, or armour. And unshod horses ridden with stirrupless
saddles were little use except as transport animals. Other
theories, with a little more justification, make Arthur a West
Country or Kentish or Lincolnshire champion; or even Count
of the Saxon Shore, repelling the invaders on the East Coast.

But closer attention to the text will reveal a rather different
state of affairs. If we omit the names of the battles, none of
which can be allocated to definite modern sites, and examine
the structure of the narrative, we find clear traces of a deliberately assembled list. Firstly, there are twelve battles. Four of
these are fought in the same place. This looks like an obvious
attempt to 'round up' to a suitable number. Might the original
inspiration for the passage have been a reference to 'the
twelve battles of Arthur'? The alternative would be a poem
listing Arthur's battles, on the analogy of the poems listing the
battles of Cadwallawn, Cynan Garwyn, Urien, Owain and
Gwallawg. This would point to a relatively widespread

7

tradition of 'battle-lists', and it does seem probable that this is the source, or at least the inspiration, of Nennius's list. The surviving poems are quite close in style – that on Cadwallawn runs:

> Cadwallawn, before his coming
> waged them for our good fortune –
> fourteen chief battles for fair Britain,*
> and sixty encounters.
>
> The camp of Cadwallawn on the Caint;
> England in trouble
> according to the prophecy of birds,
> open-handed, honour flowed (?).
>
> The camp of Cadwallawn on the Don [*or* on the wave];
> fierce affliction to his foe,
> a lion of hosts over the Saxons.
>
> The camp of Cadwallawn the famous,
> on the uplands of Mount Digoll,
> seven months and seven battles each day.
>
> The camp of Cadwallawn on the Severn,
> and on the other side of the river Dygen,
> almost burning Meigen.
>
> The camp of Cadwallawn on the Wye;
> shore after a sea-voyage
> with the arranger of the battle-location (?).
>
> The camp of Cadwallawn on Bedwyr's well;
> he acquired gifts before all warriors,
> Cynon demonstrated there the assertion of gifts.†
>
> The camp of Cadwallawn on the Taf;
> very numerous I see them,
> the skilful and strong lord.
>
> The camp of Cadwallawn on the Tawy;
> a slaying hand in the breach,
> the famous trouble-seeker.

* Sixteen are apparently listed.
† = his claim to them?

The camp of Cadwallawn beyond Caer,
a besieging army, and a hundred zealous men,
a hundred battles, and the destruction of a hundred cities.

The camp of Cadwallawn on the Cowyn;
a weary hand on the rein,
the men of England, numerous their complaints.

The camp of Cadwallawn tonight;
it is said in the dwellings on the headland [*or* Pembroke]
a thing that is a great protection, difficult to flee from it.*

The camp of Cadwallawn on the Teifi,
he mixed blood with brine,
he avenged the violence of Gwynedd.

The camp of Cadwallawn beside the waterways
he satiated eagles;
after battle, corpses their gift.

The camp of Cadwallawn, my brother
in the uplands of Dunawd's land,
his anger was fierce in battle.

The camp of Cadwallawn on the Meirin;†
a lion of hosts to the people,
a great tumult, terrible his onslaught.

By the plotting of strangers and unrighteous monks,
water flows from the fountain,
sad and heavy will be the day because of Cadwallawn.

The wood has put on the fair robes of summer,
anger that is fated will hasten;
let us meet around Elfed.

Compared with this, Nennius's text is almost too literary in its
detail. The battle of *urbs legionis* or Chester is the battle of
Chester of *c.* 616; that of Badon Hill appears in Gildas,
without the commander being named, in a very vague context.
Two others are associated with Arthur in literary sources: the

* i.e. a headland?
† Place unidentified.

Dialogue with Glewlwyd contains references to Trath Tribruit (Tryfrwyd) and perhaps, if we accept the identification of Agned and Eidyn, to the battle of 'mons Agned'. This leaves three battles on rivers, one of which (the Dubglas, or Black-water) has a name found in several different parts of the country, but not in Lincolnshire or Lennox, the two proposed identifications of 'Linnuis'; the other two defy identification, but the list recalls Guorthemir's battles on fords and river crossings. The battle 'in the forest of Celidon' is almost certainly a reference to the territory north of the Antonine wall, but is hopelessly unspecific, while Guinnion has defied all attempts to identify it with existing Roman camps. In total, there are four battles known elsewhere, three on rivers, one unspecific and one unidentified. If this is compared with the other poems mentioned, we obtain the following results:

	Total	Un-known	Genera-lized place	Identi-fiable	Also known elsewhere	Battles on rivers	Battles in forests
Arthur	9	1	1	1	4	4	1
Cadwallawn	16	2	1	13	–	7	–
Owain	4	4	–	3	1	1	–
Gwallawg	9	4	2	2	1	1	–
Urien	7	4	2	1	2	1	1
Cynan Garwyn	4	1	–	3	1	1	–

The bare outline of the battles is embellished with a number of details, which imply that the list comes from an earlier source, and that Nennius is expanding and commenting on it. He explains both the battles on the Dubglas and that in the forest of Celidon, giving the first a general location (*in regione Linnuis*), and glossing the second with its Welsh name. This process of adding the Welsh names is also found in the Vatican version, where they are also given for Agned, which is identi-fied with what appears to be the 'battle in the cells of Brewyn' in the list of Urien's battles, and for *urbs legionis* which is called

Caerleon. It would seem in both cases that notes on the text have either accidentally or deliberately become part of it.

More difficult are the major details which Nennius gives. In the eighth battle, Arthur's victory is attributed to the intervention of Christ and the Virgin, and Arthur is said to have carried the image of the Virgin on his shoulders. Despite a clever suggestion that *yscuit*, 'shield', might have been misread as *yscuid*, 'shoulders', the passage is a glaring early ninth-century addition. A detailed device on a shield of this date has yet to be found, and even in the eleventh century, devices were still extremely simple: the most complex shown on the Bayeux tapestry is a monster (and this may be imaginary, as it relates closely to the beasts in the border pattern). On the other hand, there is a long tradition of bearing crosses into battle, though even this is rare enough in the west. There is a parallel story in Bede, of the setting up of a cross before the battle of Hefenfelth, near Hexham, in the 630s:

The place is still shown today and is held in great veneration where Oswald, when he was about to engage in battle set up the sign of the holy cross and, on bended knees, prayed God to send heavenly aid to his worshippers in their dire need. In fact it is related that when a cross had been hastily made and the hole dug in which it was to stand, he seized the cross himself in the ardour of his faith, placed in the hole, and held it upright with both hands until the soldiers had heaped up the earth and fixed it in position.[23]

Is Nennius perhaps consciously setting up Arthur as a Briton rival to Oswald, who is arguably Bede's central heroic figure? It is a difficult problem, and, although most scholars have denied any knowledge of Bede on Nennius's part, it is tempting to agree with the argument that in the version we now have, Nennius added some details as a result of reading Bede.[24]

On the other hand, we still have to account for the remarkable choice of the Virgin Mary as 'patron saint'. Mariolatry developed almost entirely in the Eastern church, and spread only slowly through the west from the fifth century onwards. The majority of French and German churches dedicated to her are not earlier than the seventh century, and the major festivals associated with her cult were only introduced after the Gallican liturgy had been replaced by that of Rome towards the middle of the eighth century. Supposedly early literature on Mary often proves to be forged, such as the apocryphal *Gospel of Mary's birth and Christ's childhood* and the pseudo-Jerome discourse on Mary's assumption. At the end of the seventh century, the language used in the worship of Mary was still restrained, and there was no mention of her 'mediation'.[25]

Under the Carolingian empire, however, the picture changed very rapidly. The four great festivals of the Roman rite (Nativity, Dormition, Presentation and Purification) were introduced;[26] Alcuin, Charlemagne's Saxon mentor, instituted a Marian mass on Saturdays; and the great imperial basilica at Aix-la-Chapelle was dedicated to the Virgin. The French monasteries showed an increasing interest in Mariology, culminating in the writings of Paschasius Radbertus and Ratramnus of Corbie in the mid-ninth century. One particular phrase in Nennius is of note, the use of the title *sanctae Mariae perpetuae virginis* (holy Mary, ever-virgin); though this concept is affirmed in pseudo-Jerome and in Augustine, it is nonetheless rare before the ninth century.[27] It seems as though Nennius, or perhaps even an early copyist was in contact with a centre of Marian worship; and this centre must have been on the Continent or in England. The latter is unlikely, since although Mariolatry was established early in England (Bede wrote a poem for the feast of the nativity of the Virgin), it remained relatively restrained. In Wales itself, the evidence of Church dedications to the Virgin, all of which are either twelfth century or due to Saxon influence on the border, and of the almost total absence of the Virgin from early secular literature except in the epithet *mab Mair*, 'son of Mary', applied to our Lord,[28] shows that there was no native Marian cult at all, probably because the Celtic and Roman practices had only coincided since 768. The most probable milieu in which Nennius might have come into contact with this Marian devotion is the circle of Sedulius Scottus and his friends which we have already discussed. In the verses possibly addressed to king Rhodri, there is a reference to Mary as 'the Virgin, holding sway in high-throned paradise', and the attitudes of Carolingian France were brought across the Channel not only by these wandering Irish but by Alcuin's compatriots as well. So Frankish, Saxon or Irish scholars could have indirectly introduced this theme into Nennius's account of Arthur, but it is not a native one, and it is certainly a very recent addition, perhaps even later than Nennius's own version of the *History of the Britons*.

The other battle for which details are given is that of Badon Hill. The search for this famous battle has long exercised scholars and others; there is general agreement that it refers to one of several sites containing the element Bad- in south-west England such as Badbury Rings, a view supported by such historical data as Gildas provides. But it seems unlikely that this battle is one of Arthur's genuine exploits. The name certainly comes from Gildas, who is our only independent authority for it; and his account would also suggest that it was the last of a series of battles. Nennius's details are purely fabulous, the career of some legendary literary hero, and inspire no confidence in his solution to Gildas's greatest riddle. Nor do other sources support the idea that Badon was a victory so decisive that it was always held in reverence: it seems to have been a prelude to a local peace with the Saxons, as we have seen. But Nennius is concerned to build up Arthur's prestige and to make him a national figure; and to this end the only major battle mentioned by Gildas is employed,[29] and combined with a piece of stock poetic eulogy. Nor, apart from this one last item in a list of very mixed antecedents, is there any other evidence for an Arthur in the south of England in the late fifth century. The possibility must always remain; but it is supported only by this isolated entry, not by a consistent body of evidence such as relates to Arthur of Dalriada.

Furthermore, Nennius has a very clear motive in building up Arthur's reputation. He was writing at a time when the possibility of regaining land from the Saxons was a very real one for the first time in nearly two centuries, when the hour of the Saxons' expulsion, so carefully reckoned up by prophetic bards and even by Gildas, seemed near at hand. He emphasizes the antiquity of the British race in the history of the origins of Britain; he underlines the momentary weakness of their ruler, Vortigern, and the treachery of the Saxons which allowed the latter to gain a foothold in the island; and he shows how, despite increasing odds, the British put up a valiant and often successful resistance. But he does all this with the barest vestiges of historical material at his disposal: hints from continental writers for the genealogy, popular stories for Vortigern and Hengist, and scraps of antiquarian information for Arthur. The three narratives round which his national history is constructed are those of Gildas, who offers no more than a broad and often confused sequence, the biography of St Germanus, which covers a short period in some detail, and the 'northern history' which is itself a similarly disconnected collection. For without any real chronological information, Nennius was gravely handicapped when it came to correlating his miscellany. The laborious calculation of dates in the last chapter of the *History of the Britons*, which still defy a clear interpretation, is some indication of the problems involved: a series of events drawn from other chroniclers such as Aurelius Victor and Prosper are listed and used as a basis for an attempt at a background chronology for the whole period. The result is 'confusion worse confounded', and it is fair to say that no successful solution of the problems of dating events of the fifth and sixth centuries is likely to be achieved.

The same chronological problem occurs even more forcefully in the *Annals of Wales*, found in the same manuscript as the best copy of Nennius's *History* (British Museum Harleian 3859), which also includes the genealogies, and is an eleventh-century collection of the most important materials for Welsh history. The *Annals* are placed as though the calculation at the end of Nennius's work were their introduction. Of the eight entries on the first page, six relate to church affairs, four of them concerning Irish saints; the other two read as follows:

Year 72 The battle of Badon in which Arthur carried the cross of our Lord Jesus Christ for three days and three nights on his shoulders and the Britons were victors.
Year 93 Gueith [Battle of] Camlann, in which Arthur and Medraut died. And there was great mortality in the island.[30]

The accepted opening date for the sequence of the *Annals of Wales* is 444, giving Badon as 516 and Camlan as 537. But the style of the two entries marks them out as distinctly out of character with the rest of the material, which until about 600 is brief and couched in the vocabulary of other monastic records. The battle of Badon has been enlarged upon because of its place in Gildas's history; the detail derives from Nennius's efforts. The date is related to that of the death of Gildas, recorded in the *Annals of Wales* for 570, and seems to have been arrived at by taking the 'forty-four years' in Gildas's narrative (from the date of Badon to the time at which he wrote) and allowing a further ten years between the writing of the *De Excidio* and his death. The details of the battle are a simplified version of Nennius's narrative: the idea of an image of the Virgin being an unusual one, the chronicler has replaced it by the more familiar cross.

The second entry is of much greater interest. Firstly, the use of the Welsh word 'gueith' is unexpected in an ecclesiastical source, where the language is otherwise Latin.[31] Two other battles are similarly described, which would imply that the compiler was drawing on a vernacular list of great battles, probably without dates. The other battles are likely to have been taken ultimately from Bede, but the battle of Camlan is part of a consistent independent tradition which we have already looked at; but this is the first specific reference to Arthur's death there. It is not clear whether Arthur was fighting Medrawd or was allied to him, though the evidence of the triads suggests civil war. But once again the dating depends on the meagre data given by Gildas for Badon Hill: drawing on traditional sources with no indication of date, the chronicler has again done his best to supply a date of 'a decade after Badon'. In all this, the only original entry is that for the death of Gildas, which is derived from Irish sources (the Annals of Tigernach and Annals of Ulster), Gildas being highly regarded as a saint by the Irish.[32] The site of Camlan, like those in Nennius's list, has been variously identified, though one candidate does stand out: Birdoswald on Hadrian's Wall, which was known in Welsh as Camglann.[33] This would once more support our thesis that Arthur is the prince of Dalriada, though so far we have deliberately avoided the use of philological evidence, due to its extremely tentative nature.

By the tenth century, when the *Annals of Wales* were compiled, Arthur was well on the way to becoming established as an important figure in Welsh history, to whose glorious victories later bards would appeal when exhorting their present rulers to greater efforts against the Saxon. In the process of this conversion from a northern prince to general saviour of the nation, however, his original place and period gradually became obscured, partly because of misunderstandings, partly because of a desire to ascribe to one victorious figure one particular reference to what seemed to be the last great defeat

of the hated invader. From now on, Arthur belongs almost
entirely to legend: but there are still a few traces of the original
Arthur to be found even in the works of fiction and pseudohistory.

7 The National Messiah

Once the figure of Arthur as the last hero before the Saxon darkness descended had been established, it was to be expected that he would develop into a legendary figure. Three distinct traditions can be distinguished: the leader in war who becomes a great ruler, the secular ruler who is contrasted with the religious heroes of the Church, and the heroic figure whose exploits are the origin of place-names. In all three cases, he usurps the fame of earlier figures, some of them completely forgotten, some still distinguishable. But the diversity of his various legends argues strongly that he came to prominence without having a specific tradition attached to his name, that he was a symbolic figure, created, as we have seen, from small scraps of evidence rather than the hero of a lost saga. His powerful yet adaptable image is in large measure the reason for this continuing popularity.

The evolution from leader in war, as in Nennius, to great ruler, is not clearly defined. The gradual growth of references to him in literature as a kind of focal figure automatically endowed him with a court; for in Welsh society, it was unthinkable that a war leader should be other than a prince. Hence in the later triads the formula *llys Arthur*, 'of Arthur's court', comes to include a host of characters and episodes whose original background has been forgotten, and replaces the earlier phrase *Ynys Prydein*, 'of the Island of Britain'. The earliest references to the idea of Arthur as a great ruler is difficult to trace: the *Dialogue of Glewlwyd* only hints at Arthur as a leader, not necessarily as a ruler. The adjective 'emperor' applied to him in the elegy on Gereint is uncertain evidence, pointing to a possible amended text rather than an early tradition.

The idea of Arthur's court, which is the key to his transformation from *dux bellorum* to *imperator* first appears in the Welsh romances usually known as the *Mabinogion*, in the story of *Culhwch and Olwen*. In its present form, *Culhwch and Olwen* dates from the end of the eleventh century, and is not entirely coherent or complete. In outline the story tells how Arthur helps his nephew Culhwch to win Olwen, daughter of the giant Ysbadadden, by fulfilling the tasks which the giant sets. The tale itself is a well-known type, and many of the feats and incidents have parallels elsewhere: the outline of the story is such that any number of variations or additions can be included. The author has ransacked earlier literature, Welsh and Irish, for his episodes. Some of these confirm Arthur's earlier legendary function as leader of a war band, including Cai and Bedwyr, which performed mysterious heroic feats: the expedition to Annwn appears as a raid on Ireland, and Cai's remarkable powers are described in a vein similar to the *Dialogue with Glewlwyd*, though his actual accomplishments are rather fewer. Some sections of the tale are missing, as nineteen of the tasks set are not accomplished, while of the remaining twenty-one some are only described briefly. Arthur is engaged in fourteen of these, including one episode which constitutes a separate saga on its own: the hunting of the boar Twrch Trwyth. There are in fact two boar hunts, that of Ysgithyrwyn and that of Twrch Trwyth. The first seems to be a duplicate version of the latter, in the way that such motifs were repeated in epic cycles: there are examples in the Irish poems about Cuchulain.

The theme of Arthur as huntsman appears in both earlier and later literature: the figure of the Wild Huntsman is sometimes identified with Arthur, which has led to all kinds of mythological speculation which would make him a god of war and of the chase. But the origin of the boar-hunt stories is much simpler: they fall into the category of poems explaining the names of places, and in both cases Arthur is a local hero to whom these tales have become attached. Another version of the story is in an appendix to the *History of the Britons* on the *Marvels of Britain*; this is probably not by Nennius, even though it is possible that he could have included another independent treatise without altering it. All the marvels except the first two come from south or south-east Wales or the west country. Gwent, Somerset and the Severn are the most common sites: among the items described are the springs at Bath and the Severn bore. Two of the marvels relate to Arthur:

There is another marvel in the region called Buelt: there is a cairn of stones there and one stone placed on top of it with the track of a dog in it: when the boar Troynt was hunted, Cabal, who was the dog of Arthur the warrior, left his track on the stone, and Arthur later built a cairn under the stone on which there was his dog's track, and it is called *Carn Cabal*. And men come and bear away the stones in their hands for a day and a night and the next day they are found back on the cairn.

There is another marvel in the region called Ercing: there is there a grave near a spring called Licat Anir; and the name of the man who is buried in the tomb was called Anir; he was the son of Arthur the warrior and he himself killed him there and buried him. And men come to measure the tomb and some find it six feet long, some nine, some twelve and some fifteen; however often you measure it, it will never measure the same the second time, and I myself have tried it.[1]

This essay on marvels only appears in one group of manuscripts, and was probably added at a later date, perhaps in the tenth or eleventh century, to the original essay. The explanation of the tomb of Anir is clearly a later addition to the original description of the tumulus, which would have been no more than 'so-and-so's grave'. This gives us the key to both 'marvels': they are explanations of well-known topographical features, rather than early legends of which the place-names are relics.

Both places can still be identified: Licat Amir is at Gamber Head in Herefordshire, near the source of the river Worm, though the tumulus itself has disappeared. *Carn Cabal* is the present Corn Gafallt overlooking the upper Wye valley, where cairns and stones with marks of the type described can still be found. This, however, sheds little light on the origins of the story of Cabal. The first problem is that Cabal is plainly derived from *caballus*, late Latin for a horse, and the story should really concern Arthur's horse, particularly as *carn* can also mean hoof in old Welsh.[2] Hence the original name meant 'horse's hoof'; but with the passage of time, the allusion – one of many similar animal place-names in Wales – was forgotten, though in *Culhwch and Olwen* Cafall appears both as a dog and as the name of a horse belonging to Bwlch, Cyfwlch and Syfwlch.[7] It seems likely that the *Marvels* are later than the original story of the hunting of Twrch Trwyth, and that this identification was made afterwards: such relocations of famous stories are common, and there is no other Arthurian tradition in this area. There is no internal evidence to show that the *Marvels* are as old as the ninth century, and certain features, such as the story of St Illtud's tomb, echo the monastic saints' lives of the late eleventh century: while the hunting of Twrch Trwyth would seem to go back to seventh- or eighth-century sources.

Hence the story of Twrch Trwyth is only haphazardly linked with Corn Gafallt and the *Marvels*. It may be that Arthur's hound originally had a different though similar name, which was changed to Cabal by later writers; the version of the hunt in the *Mabinogion* is far from being the original. In the seventh-century Book of Aneirin, one poem refers to Twrch Trwyth, perhaps even to the hunting of him. And a brief reference in the *Culhwch* version to the fact that he was a king who had been changed into a swine for his wickedness suggests a much earlier story. The present version is plainly adapted from earlier material to produce a narrative explaining place-names, no difficult task in view of the number of Welsh names involving animals.[4] The route of the hunt begins in Pembrokeshire, when Twrch Trwyth lands from Ireland, and can for the most part be traced on a modern map. The surviving version runs as follows:

They set out by sea towards Wales; and Arthur and his hosts, his horses and his dogs, went aboard Prydwen, and in the twinkling of an eye they saw them. Twrch Trwyth came to land at Porth Cleis in Dyfed. That night Arthur came as far as Mynyw. On the morrow Arthur was told they had gone by, and he overtook him killing the cattle of Cynwas Cwryfagyl, after slaying what men and beasts were in Deu Gleddyf before the coming of Arthur.

From the time of Arthur's coming, Twrch Trwyth made off thence to Preseleu. Arthur and the hosts of the world came thither. Arthur sent his men to the hunt, Eli and Trachmyr, and Drudwyn the whelp of Greid son of Eri in his own hand; and Bedwyr with Arthur's dog Cafall in his hand. And he ranged all the warriors on either side the Nyfer. There came the three sons of Cleddyf Difwlch, men who had won great fame at the slaying of Ysgithyrwyn Chief Boar. And then he set out from Glyn Nyfer and came to Cwm Cerwyn, and there he stood at bay. And he then slew four of Arthur's champions, Gwarthegydd son of Caw, Tarawg of Allt Clwyd, Rheiddwn son of Eli Adfer, and Isgofan the Generous. And after he had slain those men, again he stood at bay against them there, and slew Gwydre son of Arthur, Garselit the Irishman, Glew son of Ysgawd, and Isgawyn son of Banon. And then he himself was wounded.

And the morrow's morn at point of day some of the men caught up with him. And then he slew Huandaw and Gogigwr and Penpingon, the three servants of Glewlwyd Mighty-grasp, so that God knows he had never a servant left to him in the world, save only Llaesgymyn, a man for whom none was the better. And over and above those he slew many a man of the country, and Gwlyddyn the Craftsman, Arthur's chief builder. And then Arthur caught up with him at Peluniawg, and he then slew Madawg son of Teithion, and Gwyn son of Tringad son of Neued, and Eiriawn Penlloran. And thence he went to Aber Tywi. And there he stood at bay against them, and he then slew Cynlas son of Cynan and Gwilenhin king of France. Thereafter he went to Glyn Ystun, and then the men and dogs lost him.

Arthur summoned to him Gwyn son of Nudd and asked him whether he knew aught of Twrch Trwyth. He said he did not. Thereupon all the huntsmen went to hunt the pigs as far as Dyffryn Llychwr. And Grugyn Silver-bristle and Llwydawg the Hewer dashed into them and slew the huntsmen so that not a soul of them escaped alive, save one man only. So Arthur and his hosts came to the place where Grugyn and Llwydawg were. And then he let loose upon them all the dogs that had been named to this end. And at the clamour that was then raised, and the barking, Twrch Trwyth came up and defended them. And ever since they had crossed the Irish Sea, he had not set eyes on them till now. Then was he beset by men and dogs. With might and with main he went to Mynydd Amanw, and then a pigling was slain of his pigs. And then they joined with him life for life, and it was then Twrch Llawin was slain. And then another of his pigs was slain, Gwys was his name. And he then went to Dyffryn Amanw, and there Banw and Benwig were slain. Not one of his pigs went with him alive from that place, save Grugyn Silver-bristle and Llwydawg the Hewer.

From that place they went on to Llwch Ewin, and Arthur caught up with him there. Then he stood at bay. And then he slew Echel Big-hip, and Arwyli son of Gwyddawg Gwyr, and many a man and dog besides. And after that they went on to Llwch Tawy. Grugyn Silver-bristle then parted from them, and Grugyn thereafter made for Din Tywi. And he proceeded then into Ceredigiawn, and Eli and Trachmyr with him, and a multitude along with them besides. And he came as far as Garth Grugyn. And there Grugyn was slain in their midst, and he slew Rhuddfyw Rhys and many a man with him. And then Llwydawg went on to Ystrad Yw. And there the men of Llydaw met with him, and he then slew Hir Peisawg king of Llydaw, and Llygadrudd Emys and Gwrfoddw, Arthur's uncles, his mother's brothers. And there he himself was slain.

Twrch Trwyth went then between Tawy and Ewyas. Arthur summoned Cornwall and Devon to meet him at the mouth of the Severn. And Arthur said to the warriors of this Island: 'Twrch Trwyth has slain many of my men. By the valour of men, not while I am alive shall he go into Cornwall. I will pursue him no further, but I will join with him life for life. You, do what you will.' And by his counsel a body of horsemen was sent, and the dogs of the Island with them, as far as Ewyas, and they beat back thence to the Severn, and they waylaid him there with what tried warriors there were in this Island, and drove him by sheer force into Severn. And Mabon son of Modron went with him into Severn, on Gwyn Dun-mane the steed of Gweddw, and Goreu son of Custennin and Menw son of

Teirgwaedd, between Llyn Lliwan and Aber Gwy. And Arthur fell upon him, and the champions of Britain along with him. Osla Big-knife drew near, and Manawydan son of Llyr, and Cacamwri, Arthur's servant, and Gwyngelli, and closed in on him. And first they laid hold of his feet, and soused him in Severn till it was flooding over him. On the one side Mabon son of Modron spurred his horse and took the razor from him, and on the other Cyledyr the Wild, on another horse, plunged into Severn with him and took from him the shears. But or ever the comb could be taken he found land with his feet; and from the moment he found land neither dog nor man nor horse could keep up with him until he went into Cornwall. Whatever mischief was come by in seeking those treasures from him, worse was come by in seeking to save the two men from drowning. Cacamwri, as he was dragged forth, two quernstones dragged him into the depths. As Osla Big-knife was running after the boar, his knife fell out of its sheath and he lost it; and his sheath thereafter being full of water, as he was dragged forth, it dragged him back into the depths.

Then Arthur went with his hosts until he caught up with him in Cornwall. Whatever mischief was come by before that was play to what was come by then in seeking the comb. But from mischief to mischief the comb was won from him. And then he was forced out of Cornwall and driven straight forward into the sea. From that time forth never a one has known where he went, and Aned and Aethlem with him. And Arthur went thence to Celli Wig in Cornwall, to bathe himself and rid him of his weariness.[5]

The first episodes of the story take place in Dyfed, and it is this that may give us the clue to Arthur's place in the story. The tale is clearly in an Irish tradition; and Arthur of Dyfed, with his Irish background, could easily be the hero of such a story. Furthermore, the duplicate hunting of Ysgithyrwyn Chief Boar in the north contains characters associated with Arthur of Dalriada in other legends. The two parallel tales may have suggested the relocation of Arthur in south-west Wales and later in Cornwall after his northern origins had been forgotten by popular storytellers. The process of migration of heroes from the north to a new home in the south is far from uncommon, Tristan being another example, again perhaps inspired by records of a Cornish Tristan as well. So two sets of local legends combined with Nennius's desire to create a national hero lead to this composite, magnetic figure of Arthur in the romances, attracting all kinds of totally alien material.

Some support for the way in which the two heroes merged into one is to be found in William of Malmesbury's *Deeds of the Kings of Britain* (*c.* 1125). He describes the discovery of the grave of Walwain (Gawain), Arthur's nephew, in the reign of William the Conqueror (1066–87):

At this time there was found in the province of Wales called Ros the grave of Walwen, the scarcely degenerate nephew of Arthur by his sister. He reigned in that part of Britain now called Walweitha: a warrior most renowned for his valour, but who was driven out of his kingdom by the brother and nephew of Hengist, of whom I spoke in the first book, though not before he had avenged his exile by inflicting much harm on them. He deservedly shared his uncle's fame, for they averted the ruin of their country for many years. But the tomb of Arthur is nowhere to be seen, for which reason the dirges of old relate that he is to come again. But the tomb of the other, as I have said, was found in King William's time on the sea-shore, fourteen feet long; whence some assert that he was wounded by his enemies and washed ashore in a shipwreck, some that he was killed by the citizens in a public banquet. The truth is therefore in doubt, though neither story would damage his reputation.[6]

The grave is now known as Walwyn's Castle, near Milford Haven in Pembrokeshire, having been rebuilt as the base of an early castle. Part of William's story rests on Nennius's episode of Octha and Ebissa's exploits in the north; but even so, the connection of Walwain and Galloway (Walweitha) seems to be genuine. Hence Arthur of Dalriada, not Arthur of Dyfed, is involved; but in the process of finding new locations for the heroes of the north, Walwein has been found a home in Dyfed because of his Arthurian connections; hence the conflicting traditions reported by William of Malmesbury.

The problem in demonstrating this development is that the stories of which Arthur is hero were not bound by the formal rules of bardic tradition and hence, like *The Gododdin*, preserved in something approaching their early form. Each storyteller re-worked the theme at pleasure, and the suggestion that an early story about Arthur of Dyfed lies at the basis of the boar hunt episode must remain a hypothesis. For instance, the route taken by Arthur on landing from Ireland is very similar to that taken by Gruffydd ap Cynan in 1081 with his troops.[7] And as soon as the chase moves out of south-west Wales, the narrative is no longer so clearly defined in terms of places, as though the storyteller was a stranger to the area he was describing. Furthermore, there are probably gaps in the narrative, particularly at the point where the route of the hunt might have gone northwards to include Carn Cabal, though this otherwise stands apart from the main area in which the hunt takes place.

The story of the slaying of Ysgithyrwyn Chief Boar, which precedes the hunting of Twrch Trwyth, does seem to derive from independent material. It runs as follows:

After that Arthur made his way to Llydaw, and with him Mabon son of Mellt and Gware Golden-hair, to seek the two dogs of Glythfyr Ledewig. And when he had obtained them, Arthur went to the west of Ireland to seek out Gwrgi Seferi, and Odgar son of Aedd king of Ireland along with him. And after that Arthur went into the North and caught Cyledyr the Wild; and he went after Ysgithyrwyn Chief Boar. And Mabon son of Mellt went, and the two dogs of Glythfyr Ledewig in his hand, and Drudwyn the whelp of Greid son of Eri. And Arthur himself took his place in the hunt, and Cafall, Arthur's dog, in his hand. And Cadw of Prydein mounted Llamrei, Arthur's mare, and he was the first to bring the boar to bay. And then Cadw of Prydein armed him with a hatchet, and boldly and gallantly set upon the boar and split his head in two. And Cadw took the tusk. It was not the dogs which Ysbaddaden had named to Culhwch which killed the boar, but Cafall, Arthur's own dog.[8]

Cadw or Caw appears in both the *Life of St Gildas* and the *Life of St Cadoc*, and is portrayed as a ruler from northern Britain, father of a large number of saints, including Gildas. In the *Life of St Cadoc* he is a giant, and his outlandish appearance might suggest a Pictish background, especially as he is slain in the north by a king whose lands he lays waste. The other names are all borrowed from the story of Twrch Trwyth; and the author's awareness of the confusion is betrayed by his last remark, though Ysbaddaden never actually names the dogs that are to kill Ysgithyrwyn.

A curious triad also associates Arthur with a pig-hunt of a very different kind.

Three Powerful Swineherds of the Island of Britain:
Drystan son of Tallwch, who guarded the swine of March son of Meirchiawn, while the swineherd went to ask Essyllt to come to a meeting with him. And Arthur was seeking (to obtain) one pig from among them, either by deceit or by force, but he did not get it.[9]

The episode corresponds closely with the early versions of the story of Tristan and Iseult, with its clandestine meetings. But Arthur's presence seems to be a later introduction. It is possible that a genuine association with a Tristan from the north (there are several instances of the name during the sixth and seventh centuries)[10] was later transferred to the Cornish Tristan, and was responsible for Arthur's Cornish associations: certainly the part played by Arthur in the Tristan story is very slight, and involves him in his role as lord of a great court. Kelliwic in Cornwall appears in *Culhwch and Olwen* as Arthur's Cornish capital; but no satisfactory explanation of this association has yet been offered. Another triad offers Kelliwic, Mynyw (St David's) in Dyfed and Pen Rhionydd in the north (perhaps in Galloway and therefore in Dalriadic territory) as Arthur's three courts. An alternative association which could have preserved Arthur's name in the south-west is that with Gereint of Devon,

'Gereint from the south' in *The Gododdin*; a distant memory of
their alliance in the north could have been relocated on
Gereint's own territory. At best, the problem of how Arthur's
association with Cornwall originated remains an open question.
There is no very early evidence for it, and it may belong to the
tenth or eleventh century, after his prestige had already become
considerable.

Our next source of early Arthurian legends is a curious one. In
the lives of various Welsh saints dating from the late eleventh
and early twelfth centuries, Arthur appears as a petty tyrant,
whom the saints duly chastise into repentance for his various
misdeeds. We have already used some of the material from the
Life of St Gildas,[11] which, with the *Life of St Cadoc*, is one of the
earlier surviving works in this genre. The tradition of writing
saints' lives is found both in Ireland and on the Continent from
a fairly early date; but the Welsh lives generally bear the stamp
of an attempt to supply a gap in the records of the local church.
They do contain some legendary material, but this is gleanings
from bards and storytellers rather than carefully-preserved early
records. The main centre of these antiquarian researches, not
unlike those of Nennius, was the south Welsh monasteries,
particularly Llancarfan. The object was not only to supply a
missing biography, but also to enhance the honour and prestige
of the particular foundation, and to lay claim to extensive
apocryphal grants of land made by early benefactors, a process
which is far from uncommon throughout the Middle Ages and
of which the Glastonbury monks were skilled exponents.

   The earliest of the surviving *Lives* is that of St Cadoc, written
by Lifric of Llancarfan about 1050. Arthur appears in two
episodes, both discreditable. In the first, he is sitting with Cai
and Bedwyr playing dice on top of a hill, when a soldier and a
girl appear, pursued by a host of armed men. Arthur declares
that he is 'violently inflamed by desire for the girl', but his com-

panions dissuade him, saying that 'we are in the habit of helping those in need or distress'. So the three of them hold the pursuers at bay and allow the couple to escape. From their marriage St Cadoc is born; and Arthur encounters him many years later when Ligessauc Llawhir, having slain three of Arthur's soldiers, seeks sanctuary with the saint. The saint succeeds in mediating between Arthur and Ligessauc, but Arthur will only accept the compensation of three hundred cattle in the form of 'cows distinctly coloured, red in front and white behind'. The saint collects a hundred ordinary cows, and changes them into those of the desired colour; but when they are driven to Arthur across a ford, they change into bundles of fern. Arthur duly repents of his obstinacy, and submits to the saint.

Parts of the story come from literary traditions. Ligessauc Llawhir is the same as Llynghessawl Law Hael, 'the fleet-owner of the generous hand', who occurs in a triad as husband of one of the three faithful wives of the Island of Britain; Cai and Bedwyr are the usual companions of Arthur in the early poems. The rest is largely place-name material: Gwynlluir, Cadoc's father, is the founder of Gwynllwg, a kingdom in Glamorgan, while the whole episode of the transformation of the cows derives from the place-names Tref redinauc (fern homestead) and Reth Guurtebou (the ford of the pleading), in modern spelling Tredunnock and Rhyd Gwrthebau, and is simply an invention to account for them, using a primitive episode involving cattle borrowed from the stock situations of the early stories.

Arthur appears as a dragon-slayer in the *Life of St Carannog*, perhaps an echo of his exploits in dispatching other monsters in the secular tales; and his reputation as both dragon and giant slayer was to increase during the following century as his name was attached to episodes belonging to other heroes. For example, in Geoffrey of Monmouth's *History of the Kings of Britain*, the killing of the giant Ritho by Arthur is clearly based on the killing of Dillus Varvawc by Cai in *Culhwch and Olwen*.

The elimination of earlier heroes and their replacement by more recent favourites is a commonplace of the development of the later romances, where Galahad replaces Perceval in the Grail quest and Lancelot ousts Gawain as the most polished of Arthur's knights. Likewise Arthur himself, at this earlier and less clearly recorded period, ousts other, older heroes.

Elsewhere, Arthur's appearance is designed simply to enhance the saint's standing, as in the *Life of St Gildas*, where the abduction of Gwenhwyfar by Melvas is brought in to explain how certain lands were granted to the saint as a reward. In the *Life of St Padarn* Arthur attempts to steal the saint's tunic, and is promptly swallowed up by the earth; only by making an abject submission does he escape.

The collections of saints' lives and of saints' genealogies are further evidence of the interest of the Welsh in antiquarian matters, as well as of their readiness to supply any missing material. If the initial impetus was a desire to glorify a particular patron saint, the later complete collections such as that of the *Lives of the Welsh Saints*, made about 1120–30 on the Welsh marches, were partly due to Anglo-Norman interest in Welsh affairs which culminated in the twelfth century with Gerald of Wales's books about his country and, in Arthurian matters, Geoffrey of Monmouth's *History of the Kings of Britain*. These works stand at the end of a long tradition of antiquarian research, and the earlier Arthurian material bears continuous traces of its results. It is this distinction, between the bardic preservation of early names and stories from sixth- and seventh-century history, and the use of this material by historians or storytellers with definite views to advance, that must always be borne in mind. It means that Nennius must be viewed with strong suspicion, and that the Welsh poetry after him is a changing rather than a static tradition, adapting to meet the demands for a national myth which had triggered off Nennius's work. Only in the genealogies, the early heroic poems and the

Irish annals with their long undisturbed history is the content reliable and free from this pervasive reworking.

But the rewriting of early history had still a long way to go at the end of the eleventh century. Popular belief, monastic zeal and nationalist history all had new uses for Arthur, and it is to these that we now turn. If there is nothing to be gleaned of the historical Arthur from them, the processes by which the figure of Arthur was transmitted from history to myth can still be illuminated by these last and most extravagant efforts.

8 Popular Beliefs

We have now reached the point at which the varying shapes of the figure of Arthur are all determined by his artificial role as the national hero of Wales *par excellence*. In one form he becomes the Welsh messiah, the warrior who will come to overthrow the Saxons and Normans; in another, he becomes the emperor of a golden age; and in the third, the presiding genius of the Welsh and Cornish landscape. It is from these strands, rather than the more artificial threads of the romances, that the popular image of Arthur has been woven, an image which persists to the present day.

The idea of the returning hero is a common one in the medieval world, where some degree of primitive awe was still attached to the ruler's person. A great prince's personality would stamp itself on the imagination of his followers to the extent that his death seemed unimaginable. Charlemagne, Frederick Barbarossa and Arthur all share this distinction, and the theme belongs to folklore rather than to primitive religious belief. There is no hint of an otherworld about Barbarossa's survival, any more than in the reports of Hitler's survival. Yet it is remarkable that a figure of tradition rather than real life should acquire this charisma. An explanation is possibly to be found in the uncertainty about his death, a factor common to Barbarossa (and Hitler) as well; Barbarossa was drowned near Seleucia in Turkey in 1190, on the Third Crusade, and his body was buried at Antioch, well beyond the ken of most of his subjects. The difficult passage in the *Stanzas of the Graves*, even if it did not originally mean that Arthur's grave was unknown, may have been interpreted in this way in the tenth or eleventh century. Furthermore, Welsh prophetic verse of the period such as the *Armes Prydein* of *c.* 930 looked forward to the day of deliverance from the Saxons under heroes from the past who would return to lead their people to victory, in this case Cynan and Cadwaladr, neither of them characters likely to be known to the humbler storytellers unfamiliar with the intricacies of bardic lore. Cadwaladr remains a puzzling figure today, and his place as a deliverer can best be explained by a confusion with his father Cadwallawn. By the usual process of displacement, Arthur has taken over, in the popular imagination, the part of these two lesser known heroes, perhaps as a result of the passage in the *Stanzas of the Graves*.

The earliest record of this belief confirms our theory by specifically saying that it was a belief held among the common people. In 1113 a group of canons from Laon came over to England to raise funds to rebuild their church, burnt down in the previous year: with them they brought the miracle-working relics of the Virgin; and they travelled for some weeks in the south and west of England. When they came to Cornwall they were shown King Arthur's chair and oven near Bodmin, and soon afterwards the subject of the Welsh hero came up again:

There was a certain man with a withered hand, who was keeping watch at the shrine to benefit from its holiness. But, in the way that the Britons often argue with the French about King Arthur, this man began to argue with one of our clerks, Haganellus by name, who was of the household of Guido, archdeacon of Laon, saying that Arthur still lived. This led to no small riot, several armed men burst into the church, and if Algardus . . . had not prevented them, it might well have come to bloodshed. We believe that this quarrel before her shrine displeased our Lady; for the man with the withered hand, who started the riot because of Arthur, was not cured.[1]

The account of this journey was written down some thirty years later by Hermann of Laon but he seems to have worked from firsthand accounts: nor would there be any possible motive for inventing this curious incident. On the other hand, the comment 'in the way that the Britons often argue with the French about King Arthur' may reflect the more general interest in Arthur in his own day following the appearance of

Geoffrey of Monmouth's work in the 1130s. Whether he means by 'Britons' and 'French', Bretons and Normans or Welsh and Anglo-French is difficult to determine, though, writing at Laon, it is more likely to be the former; but this does not affect the main point, which is that belief in Arthur's return was very strong in Cornwall early in the twelfth century.

The next reference to the idea of his return is only a decade later, in William of Malmesbury's *Deeds of the Kings of the English*, in the passage already quoted: 'But the tomb of Arthur is nowhere to be seen, for which reason the dirges of old relate that he is to come again.' The *Stanzas of the Graves* might well be described as 'a dirge of old', but this would only account for the first part of William's statement. In the whole passage about Walwen and Arthur, he seems to be relying on another source, perhaps an oral one such as an interpreter who knew Welsh, and to be using his own knowledge of Nennius to amplify his original material.

The theme of Arthur's return was elaborated by Geoffrey of Monmouth about 1130 in his *History of the Kings of Britain*, that vast compendium of random Welsh folklore reshaped into a semblance of history. Though many early traditions survive in his pages, they are so often out of context or deliberately adapted, that it is impossible to set any value on them; and after his success, no subsequent Arthurian material can ever be regarded as wholly free of his influence. On the one hand, there is the development from pseudohistory into literary legend; on the other, Geoffrey's efforts bemused scholars and historical writers for many centuries. Even at the end of the nineteenth century works which took Geoffrey's account of Arthur seriously were still appearing. It was Geoffrey who elevated Arthur into the emperor of half Europe, a precursor to Charlemagne, developing Nennius's theme of the warrior-hero into unheard-of proportions, until the Arthurian armies marched on Rome itself. This vision was accepted by the historians of the Middle

Ages, and only in the revival of critical historical studies in the sixteenth century was the vast imaginary edifice demolished.

Geoffrey drew some of his material from existing topographical material: the ruins of Caerleon-upon-Usk inspired him to make it Arthur's court, and other remains and inscriptions seem to have served as the germ for his stories. But, ironically, he himself was not directly responsible for Arthur's association with the most famous of all Arthurian sites, Glastonbury, though the connection developed from the narrative of Arthur's death in the *History of the Kings of Britain*: at the end of the battle of Camlan, Geoffrey says: 'But the renowned king Arthur was mortally wounded and was borne thence to the Isle of Avalon for his wounds to be healed.' Where Geoffrey got his *'insula Avallonis'* from is still a matter of controversy: it is unknown as a place in old Welsh sources, though it has been connected with a man's name, Aballach, father of Modron, who appears as the ruler of Avalon in Geoffrey's *Life of Merlin*. On the other hand, it may be derived from the Welsh *afallenau*, 'apple trees', and could be a reference to the paradise in the west of Irish legend, or even, given Geoffrey's classical background, to the isles of the Hesperides; certainly the descriptions of it in the *Life of Merlin* would bear this out:

The island of apples which men call 'The Fortunate Isle' gets its name from the fact because it produces all things of itself; the fields there have no need of the ploughs of the farmers and all cultivation is lacking except what nature provides. Of its own accord it produces grain and grapes, and apple trees grow in its woods from the close-clipped grass. The ground of its own accord produces everything instead of merely grass, and people live there a hundred years or more. There nine sisters rule by a pleasing set of laws those who come to them from our country. She who is first of them is more skilled in the healing art, and excels her sisters in the beauty of her person. Morgen is her name, and she has learned what useful properties all the herbs contain, so that she can cure sick bodies. She also knows an art by which to change her shape, and to cleave the air on new wings like Daedalus; when she wishes she is at Brest, Chartres, or Pavia, and when she wills she slips down from the air onto your shores. And men say that she had taught mathematics to her sisters, Moronoe, Mazoe, Gliten, Glitonea, Gliton, Tyronoe; Thitis, Thitis best known for her cither. Thither after the battle of Camlan we took the wounded Arthur, guided by Barinthus to whom the waters and the stars of heaven were well known. With him steering the ship we arrived there with the prince, and Morgen received us with fitting honor, and in her chamber she placed the king on a golden bed and with her own hand she uncovered his honorable wound and gazed at it for a long time. At length she said that health could be restored to him if he stayed with her for a long time and made use of her healing art. Rejoicing, therefore, we entrusted the king to her and returning spread our sails to the favoring winds.[2]

This delightful piece of classical pastiche, however, was the precursor of a rather different version of Arthur's last resting place. The question of Arthur's return was not only a point of debate between Celts and Normans: it was a rallying-point for Celtic ambitions, a topic which Geoffrey, hoping for advancement in the Norman church, had discreetly to suppress. These beliefs were still strong at the end of the century, as the Plantagenets well knew: one of the reasons why John had Prince Arthur put to death in 1203 was fear of the magnetism of his nature as leader of a hostile Breton force. And they were certainly not displeased when Avalon and Arthur were identified and his grave opened to the world – or so the monks of Glastonbury claimed.

The fullest account of the discovery of this grave, which took place in 1190 or 1191, is given by Gerald of Wales two years later, and is worth quoting in full:

Arthur the famous British king is still remembered, nor will this memory die out, for he is much praised in the history of the excellent monastery of Glastonbury, of which he himself was in his time a distinguished patron and a generous endower and supporter . . . His body, for which popular stories have invented a fantastic ending, saying that it had been carried to a remote place, and was not subject to death, was found in recent times at Glastonbury between two stone pyramids standing in the burial ground. It was deep in the earth, enclosed in a hollow oak, and the discovery was accompanied by wonderful and almost miraculous signs. It was reverently transferred to the church and placed in a marble tomb. And a leaden cross was found laid under a stone, not above, as is the custom today, but rather fastened on beneath it. We saw this, and traced the inscription which was not showing, but turned in towards the stone: 'Here lies buried the famous king Arthurus with Wennevereia his second wife in the isle of Avallonia.' In this there are several remarkable things: he had two wives, of which the last was buried at the same time as him, and indeed her bones were discovered with those of her husband; however, they were separate, since two parts of the coffin, at the head, were divided off, to contain the bones of a man, while the remaining third at the foot contained the bones of a woman set apart. There was also uncovered a golden tress of hair that had belonged to a beautiful woman, in its pristine condition and colour, which, when a certain monk eagerly snatched it up, suddenly dissolved into dust. Signs that the body had been buried here were found in the records of the place, in the letters inscribed on the pyramids, although these were almost obliterated by age, and in the visions and revelations seen by holy men and clerks; but chiefly through Henry II, King of England, who had heard from an aged British singer that his [Arthur's] body would be found at least sixteen feet deep in the earth, not in a stone tomb, but in a hollow oak. This Henry had told the monks; and the body was at the depth stated and almost concealed, lest, in the event of the Saxons occupying the island, against whom he had fought with so much energy in his lifetime, it should be brought to light; and for that reason, the inscription on the cross which would have revealed the truth, was turned inwards to the stone, to conceal at that time what the coffin contained, and yet inform other centuries. What is now called Glastonbury was in former times called the Isle of Avallon, for it is almost an island, being entirely surrounded by marshes, whence it is named in British Inis Avallon, that is the apple-bearing island, because apples (in British aval) used to abound in that place. Whence Morgan, a noblewoman who was ruler of that region and closely related to Arthur, after the Battle of Kemelen carried him away to the island now called Glastonbury to be healed of his wounds. It

used also to be called in British Inis Gutrin, that is, the isle of glass;
hence the Saxons called it Glastingeburi. For in their tongue glas
means glass,* and a camp or town is called buri. We know that the
bones of Arthur's body that were discovered were so large that in
this we might see the fulfilment of the poet's words:

Grandiaque effossis mirabitur ossa sepulchris.†

The thigh bone, when placed next to the tallest man present, as the
abbot showed us, and fastened to the ground by his foot, reached
three inches above his knee. And the skull was of a great, indeed
prodigious, capacity, to the extent that the space between the brows
and between the eyes was a palm's breadth. But in the skull there
were ten or more wounds which had all healed into scars with the
exception of one, which made a great cleft, and seemed to have been
the sole cause of death.[3]

His account is confirmed in outline by Ralph of Coggeshall
in his *English Chronicle* some thirty years later:

1191: This year were found at Glastonbury the bones of the most
renowned Arthur, formerly King of Britain, buried in a very ancient
coffin, about which two ancient pyramids had been built: on the sides
of these was in inscription, illegible on account of the rudeness of
the script and its worn condition. The bones were discovered as
follows: as they were digging up this ground to bury a monk who
had urgently desired in his lifetime to be interred there, they discovered a certain coffin, on which a leaden cross had been placed,
bearing the inscription, 'Here lies the famous king Arturius,
buried in the isle of Avallon.' For this place, which is surrounded
by marshes, was formerly called the isle of Avallon, that is, the isle
of apples.[4]

But there is between the two versions an important dis-
crepancy, which leads us to question the authenticity of the
discovery. Gerald of Wales quotes the words on the cross
as 'Hic iacet sepultus inclytus rex Arthurus cum Wenneveria
uxore sua secunda in insula Avallonia'. He repeats it in the

* In Latin it is vitrum.
† When the graves are opened, they shall marvel at the great size of the
bones. (Virgil, *Georgics I*, 497.)

Speculum Ecclesiae twenty-five years later as: 'Hic iacet sepultus inclytus rex Arthurius in insula Avallonia cum uxore sua secunda Wenneveria.'* But Ralph of Coggeshall, although possibly relying on hearsay, while Gerald had seen the cross himself, quotes words that agree more closely with later writers: 'Hic iacet inclitus rex Arturius, in insula Avallonis sepultus.' Leland in the early sixteenth century gives: 'Hic iacet sepultus inclitus rex Arturius in insula Avalonia' from a copy of the original. He also gives from another source claiming to be an eyewitness description by one Simon of Abingdon the very different 'Hic iacet gloriosissimus rex Britonum Arturus'. Finally, Camden, from whose *Britannia* in the 1610 edition the illustration of the cross is taken, agrees with Leland and Ralph of Coggeshall: 'Hic iacet sepultus inclitus rex Arturius in insula Avalonia.'

Cross found on Arthur's grave, according to Camden's Britannia, *1610*

* The description of Guinevere as his second wife may come from the legend of the true and false Guineveres, which is of Welsh origin, and was current about this time (cf. Vulgate Merlin, *c.* 1230).

9

What are we to make of this confusion? There is little doubt
that Leland and Camden are quoting accurately what they saw
on the copy of the cross which still existed in their day. Camden
says of his illustration, '. . . which inscription or epitaph, as it
was sometime exemplified and drawn out of the first copie in
the Abbey of Glascon, I thought good for the antiquitie of the
characters here to put downe. The letters being made after a
barbarous maner, and resembling the Gothish character,
bewray plainly the barbarism of that age . . .'[5]

It is clearly stated that the cross in Glastonbury Abbey is the
'first copie'. If he means by this the original cross, then our
earliest witness is strangely inaccurate; it is far more probable
that this is a second version, in which case deliberate alterations
have been made. The lettering presents particular problems.
It is not unlike ninth-century inscriptions in style; but why
should the cross have been made in that period? It seems more
likely that someone deliberately worked from an old source;
and this could be either the thirteenth-century monks or Camden's informant.* If either assumption be correct, the disin-
terment was staged by the Glastonbury monks.

When we turn to the other aspects of the question, this
suspicion is confirmed. There is confusion over the dating:
Gerald of Wales in his first account gives no actual year;
but in his second, he says that it was in the reign of Henry II
which ended in July 1189, and in the abbacy of Henry of Sully,
appointed in the following autumn! Ralph of Coggeshall puts
it in 1191, two years later; although the news would scarcely
have travelled so slowly as this, a year earlier might be possible
without directly contradicting his evidence. Adam of Domerham gives it as 648 years after Arthur's death, which, if he
followed Geoffrey of Monmouth's date for the battle of Cam-

---

* For an example of the difficulties in dealing with Tudor drawings of
archaeological material, see T. Kendrick, *British Antiquity* (London, 1950),
pp. 162-3, where three variant versions of the Doniert stone are illustrated.

lan, would be 1190. This is a peculiar lack of consistency over a recent date, even though medieval chronicles are never exceptionally accurate.

A large number of forgeries of charters and other documents, as well as the interpolations in William of Malmesbury's *On the Antiquity of Glastonbury*, which are now generally recognized as such, but which have long confused the issue, date from this decade onwards. The interpolations, which apparently make the claim that Arthur was buried at Glastonbury before the exhumation of 1190 confirmed it, are now dated at about 1250. As to the details of the actual digging, Adam of Domerham, writing the Abbey history a century later, with access to Abbey records, may have unintentionally given us the final clue as to the true nature of the incident when he says that on the day the work began, the spot was surrounded by curtains on the abbot's orders.

An interesting possibility is raised by the mention of a 'hollow oak' in Gerald's account. It may be that in digging a new tomb in the cemetery a genuine primitive burial of the dug-out type was discovered, of the type described by C. F. C. Hawkes:

The earlier Northern Bronze Age, indeed, shows the beginning of more than one new departure in the cult of the dead ... The bodies were probably deposited in them [i.e. timber houses] in tree-trunk coffins, and inhumation ... in such coffins was already starting to be practised in Schleswig-Holstein in the beginnings of its Bronze Age ... The same rite of boat- or coffin-burial appears simultaneously in Britain in the middle centuries of the second millennium, when the North Sea trade-route was flourishing as already described, penetrating the Wessex culture along the south coast, where the burial at Hove ... was of this type, but more prominent on the east coast, especially in Yorkshire, where the Irish route over the Pennines reached the sea. The classic example is the Gristhorpe coffin-burial near Scarborough, but the recent discovery in the great barrow of Loose Howe on the Cleveland Moors of a primary burial with no less than three boat dug-outs must henceforward stand at the head of the series, and serve to show how the same rite took hold among the seafarers on both sides of the North Sea between about 1600 and 1400 BC.[6]

The actual site of the 'burial' was apparently revealed by excavations in 1962, though the results of these do not seem to have been published in full; it would be almost impossible to determine whether the 'disturbance' then found related to the removal of a particular type of burial. But Glastonbury's earlier history almost certainly included a period as a pagan sanctuary, with which such a hollowed oak burial might be associated, particularly as the nearby lake village seems to have been an important trading centre.

Nor is a good motive for such a staged discovery lacking. Arthur's grave was an obvious attraction for pilgrims, and pilgrims were the abbey's chief source of income apart from its properties. They were the only source from which large additional sums could be raised; and there was need of extra funds. In 1184, the buildings had been largely burnt down; but Henry II had provided the money for reconstruction. However, when he died in 1189 and Richard came to the throne, the Exchequer's resources were directed entirely to the fitting-out of the Crusade, and the supply of funds ceased. It is strange that within a few months of this, a new source of revenue should suddenly appear. Politically too, it would suit Richard; for the hope of Arthur's return could be used to foment rebellion in Wales, and this discovery seemed to dispose of it. Gerald tells us that Henry told the monks something about Arthur being buried at Glastonbury; this may be an oblique reference to a hint from Henry that such a discovery would be an acceptable return for his patronage.

Any discussion of the Glastonbury burial will, inevitably, like discussion of the historical Arthur, end without definite conclusion being reached. But the circumstantial evidence seems strong enough for us to say that there is not much doubt that the coffin and its contents, or at least its connection with Arthur, were produced by the monks in order to raise the money for the rebuilding of the Abbey, which, forgery or no forgery, it certainly did. Nor need all medieval monks be regarded as better in this respect than their secular contemporaries.

Whatever the monks found, the operation as a whole failed to have the desired effect. A large number of references by later writers show that the legend of Arthur's return persisted: even Malory knew the popular belief, though he was cautious about it:

Yet some men say in many parts of Inglonde that Kynge Arthure ys nat dede, but had by the wyll of oure Lorde Jesu into another place; and men say that he shall com agayne, and he shall wynne the Holy Crosse. Yet I woll nat say that hit shall be so, but rather I wolde sey: here in thys worlde he chaunged hys lyff.

Then as a last twist, even the burial at Glastonbury becomes part of the idea of his return:

And many men say that there ys wrytten upon the tumbe thus:
HIC IACET ARTHURUS, REX QUONDAM REXQUE FUTURUS[7]
[Here lies Arthur, once king, who shall be king again]

Because the basis of the 'Breton hope' of Arthur's return was irrational, it was proof against logical attacks. The monks, though they grew rich enough, did not reap the full harvest of their cunning until they had embroidered the legend with Joseph of Arimathea as well: perhaps it was they who adapted the inscription to include the possibility of his return. The original inscription identifying the bodies is given in two different versions, and the leaden cross which survived until the eighteenth century as that found in the tomb had yet another variation. A fourth would be far from impossible.

If the Glastonbury burial has little enough connection with

Arthur, Camelot, both in its medieval and modern form, has even less. The name first appears as that of Arthur's court in a late twelfth-century romance, Chrétien de Troyes's *Lancelot*, and the Welsh and Latin sources only mention it after the beginning of the thirteenth century, when they are based on the French romances. Chrétien seems to have got the name from Camulodunum, the Roman name for Colchester, perhaps from reading Pliny's *Natural History*,[8] and he certainly never intended his reader to make the identification. But if Camelot exists anywhere other than in the poet's inward vision, it is as Colchester. Malory identifies it with Winchester, in pursuit of his own private revision of the geography of the romances, which he always tried to reconcile with reality.

The most recent popular identification of Camelot, as Cadbury Castle in Somerset, is another instance of arbitrary identification. Cadbury Castle was first recorded as being called Camelot by John Leland in the sixteenth century, though he offers no grounds for the name. His description runs as follows:

At the very south ende of the chirch of South-Cadbyri standith Camallate, sumtyme a famose toun or castelle, apon a very torre or hille, wunderfully enstrengtheid of nature, to the which be 2 enteringes up by a very stepe way: one by north est, and another by south west.

The very roote of the hille whereon this forteres stode is more then a mile in cumpace.

In the upper parte of the coppe of the hille be 4. diches or trenches, and a balky waulle of yerth betwixt every one of them. In the very toppe of the hille above al the trenchis is *magna area* or *campus* of a 20. acres or more by estimation, wher yn dyverse places men may se fundations and *rudera* of walles. There was much dusky blew stone that people of the villages therby hath caryid away.

This top withyn the upper waulle is xx. acres of ground and more, and hath bene often plowid and borne very good corne.

Much gold, sylver and coper of the Romaine coynes hath be found ther yn plouing: and lykewise in the feldes in the rootes of this hille, with many other antique thinges, and especial by este.

Ther was found *in hominum memoria* a horse shoe of sylver at
Camallate.

The people can telle nothing ther but that they have hard say
that Arture much resortid to Camalat.

The old Lord Hungreford was owner of this Camallat. Now
Hastinges the Erle of Huntendune by his mother.

Diverse villages there about bere the name of Camalat by an
addition, as Quene-Camallat, and other.

The hylle and the diches kepe well now viij. shepe.

Al the ground by south west, and west of Camalat lyith in a vale,
so that one or 2. wayes it may be sene far of.[9]

Leland betrays the reason for the original association of Cadbury and Camelot: the fortuitous presence nearby of a village
named Camel, from the early form Cantmael found as far back
as the tenth century. 'Queen's' refers to Edward I's gift of it
to his wife in 1284.

So the name Camelot in connection with Cadbury is wholly
wide of the mark, even in the general sense of Arthur's court.
Nor is the enthusiastic description of the discoveries made by
the recent excavations there as 'Arthurian' warranted.

Firstly, Arthur is assumed, on evidence which even the most
ardent supporters of the idea of a fifth-century commander can
only call 'not proven', to have been the only military figure of
note in the fifth century. Secondly, the work done so far
suggests that the buildings at Cadbury of this period, such as
they are, are appropriate to a prince. If Arthur is to be accepted
as a fifth-century figure – an argument which relies on Nennius
– we have to accept also the comment 'but he himself was
leader in battles', implying that he was distinctly not a British
prince, and hence unlikely to have had a hall of the imposing
size of that traced at Cadbury. A much more likely – but
less glamorous – candidate would be a prince such as the
five kings mentioned by Gildas: Maelgwn, Aurelius Caninus,
Constantine, Vortigern and Cuneglasus. Of these Constantine,
prince of Devon, is known to have had territory nearest

Cadbury, but Gildas does not necessarily include all the princes of that region.

In any case, the argument we have already set out would show that Arthur was neither a fifth-century hero, nor associated with southern Britain. As to the 'Arthurian fact' which has been used to replace the figure of Arthur by advocates of a south British chieftain leading a resistance to the Saxons, this might better be rechristened the 'Ambrosian fact' after the far more tangible Ambrosius Aurelianus. The figure of Arthur is not to be found in a fully-fledged hero, springing unheralded from the disorganized and demoralized people which Gildas vividly portrays, but in a gradual development from a lesser, though still distinguished, figure in the north, who, through a coincidence of name and through the contraction of British territory and an accompanying coalescing of their history, was transferred in the eighth century to Wales itself. There, in an atmosphere of national resurgence, he was transformed into the pseudo-historical and legendary figure who has held men's imaginations ever since.

SELECT BIBLIOGRAPHY

List of Abbreviations

BBCS   *Bulletin of the Board of Celtic Studies*

BBSIA   *Bulletin bibliographique de la société internationale arthurienne*

Celt and Saxon   *Celt and Saxon: Studies in the early British border*, ed. Nora K. Chadwick, Cambridge 1963

Dickins Studies   *The Anglo Saxons: studies in some aspects of their history and culture presented to Bruce Dickins*, ed. Peter Clemoes, London 1959

EHR   *English Historical Review*

Neues Archiv   *Neues Archiv der Gesellschaft für altere Deutsche Geschichtskunde*

O'Donnell Lectures   *O'Donnell Lectures: Angles and Britons*, Cardiff 1963

PMLA   *Publications of the Modern Languages Association of America*

SEBC   *Studies in the Early British Church*, ed. Nora K. Chadwick, Cambridge 1958

SEBH   *Studies in Early British History*, ed. Nora K. Chadwick, Cambridge 1954

THSC   *Transactions of the Honourable Society of Cymmrodrion*

ZCP   *Zeitschrift für Celtische Philologie*

ALCOCK, LESLIE, 'By South Cadbury that is Camelot . . . ' *Antiquity*, xli, 1967, 50–3

ALCOCK, LESLIE, *Arthur's Britain*, London 1971

ANDERSON, ALAN ORR and ANDERSON, MARJORIE OGILVIE (ed. and tr.), *Adomnan's Life of Columba*, London and New York 1961

ANDERSON, ALAN ORR and ANDERSON, MARJORIE OGILVIE, 'The Dating Passage in Gildas' *Excidium*', *Scottish Historical Review*, xxv, 1928, 384–5

ANDERSON, ALAN ORR and ANDERSON, MARJORIE OGILVIE, 'Gildas and Arthur', *Celtic Review*, viii, 1912–13, 149–65

BARING-GOULD, S. and FISHER, JOHN, *The Lives of the British Saints*, Cymmrodrion Society, London 1907–13

BARTRUM, PETER C., 'Was there a British "Book of Conquests"?', *BBCS*, xxiii, 1968, 1–5

BARTRUM, PETER C., *Early Welsh Genealogical Tracts*, Cardiff 1966

BEISSEL, STEPHAN, *Geschichte der Verehrung Marias in Deutschland während des Mittelalters*, Freiburg im Breisgau 1909

BIRLEY, ROBERT, 'The Battle of Mount Badon', *Antiquity*, vi, 1932, 459–63

BLAIR, PETER HUNTER, 'The Bernicians and their Northern Frontier', *SEBH*, 137–72

BRODEUR, ARTHUR G., 'Arthur Dux Bellorum', *University of California Publications in English*, iii, 1939, 273–84 (reviewed by W. A. Nitze, *Modern Language Notes*, lvii, 1942, 64–8)

BROMWICH, RACHEL, 'The Character of the Early Welsh Tradition', *SEBH*, 83–136

BROMWICH, RACHEL, 'The Historical Triads: with special reference to Peniarth MS 16', *BBCS*, xii, 1946, 1–15

BROMWICH, RACHEL, 'Scotland and the Earliest Arthurian Tradition', *BBSIA*, xv, 1963, 85–95

BROMWICH, RACHEL, ed., *Trioedd Ynys Prydein: The Welsh Triads*, Cardiff 1961

BRÜNING, GERTRUD, 'Adamnans Vita Columbae und Ihre Ableitungen', *ZCP*, ii, 1917, 213–304

BULLOCK-DAVIES, CONSTANCE, 'Lanval and Avalon', *BBCS*, xxiii, 1969, 128–42

BULLOCK-DAVIES, CONSTANCE, *Professional Interpreters and the Matter of Britain*, Cardiff 1966

BURKITT, F. C., 'The Bible of Gildas', *Revue bénédictine*, xlvi, 1934, 206–15

BU'LOCK, J. D., 'Vortigern and the Pillar of Eliseg', *Antiquity*, xxxiv, 1960, 40–53

CHADWICK, H. M., *Early Scotland*, Cambridge 1949

CHADWICK, H. M., 'The End of Roman Britain', *SEBH*, 9–20

CHADWICK, H. M., 'The Foundation of the Early British Kingdoms', *SEBH*, 47–60

CHADWICK, H. M., 'Vortigern' (with notes by N. K. Chadwick), *SEBH*, 21–46

CHADWICK, H. MUNRO and KERSHAW, N., *The Growth of Literature*, vol. i: *The Ancient Literatures of Europe*, Cambridge 1932

CHADWICK, NORA K., *The Age of the Saints in the Early Celtic Church*, London and New York 1961

CHADWICK, NORA K., 'The Celtic Background of Anglo-Saxon England', *Yorkshire Celtic Studies*, iii, 1940–46, 13–32

CHADWICK, NORA K., 'The Celtic Background of Early Anglo-Saxon England', *Celt & Saxon*, 323–52

CHADWICK, NORA K., *Celtic Britain* (Ancient Peoples and Places 34), London and New York 1963

CHADWICK, NORA K., 'Early Culture and Learning in North Wales', *SEBC*, 29–120

CHADWICK, NORA K., 'The Lost Literature of Celtic Scotland', *Scottish Gaelic Studies*, vii, 1953, 115–83

CHADWICK, NORA K., 'Intellectual contacts between Britain and Gaul in the Fifth Century', *SEBH*, 189–263

CHADWICK, OWEN, 'The Evidence of Dedications in the Early History of the Welsh Church', *SEBH*, 173–88

CHAMBERS, E. K., *Arthur of Britain*, London 1927, rptd Cambridge and New York 1964 (reviewed by Kemp Malone, *Modern Language Notes*, xliii, 1928, 481–4)

CHAMBERS, R. W., 'Geoffrey of Monmouth and the Brut as sources of Early British History', *History*, iii, 1919, 225–8; iv, 1920, 34–45

COLGRAVE, BERTRAM and MYNORS, R. A. B., ed. and tr., *Bede's Ecclesiastical History of the English People*, Oxford 1969

COPLEY, GORDON J., *The Conquest of Wessex in the Sixth Century*, London 1954

COLLINGWOOD, W. G., 'Arthur's Battles', *Antiquity*, iii, 1929, 292–8

COURSON, AURELIEN DE, *Cartulaire de l'Abbaye de Redon*, Paris 1863

CRAWFORD, O. G. S., 'Arthur and his Battles', *Antiquity*, ix, 277–91

CRAWFORD, O. G. S., 'King Arthur's Last Battle', *Antiquity*, v, 1931, 236–9

CROSS, TOM PEETE, 'The Passing of Arthur', *Manly Anniversary Studies*, 1923, 284–94

DEMPF, ALOIS, 'Beda und die Entstehung der Artussage', *Zeitschrift für deutsche Geistesgeschichte*, i, 1935, 304–10

DILLON, MYLES and CHADWICK, NORA K., *The Celtic Realms*, London 1967

DIVERRES, P., 'Camlan', *BBCS*, vii, 1933–35, 273–4

DOMERHAM, ADAM OF, *Historia de rebus gestis glastoniensibus*, ed. Thomas Hearne, Oxford 1726

DUCHESNE, L., *Christian Worship: its origin and evolution*, tr. M. L. McClure, London 1903

EMANUEL, HYWEL D., 'An Analysis of the Composition of the "Vita Cadoci"', *National Library of Wales Journal*, vii, 1951–52, 217–27

ERDMANN, CARL, *Die Entstehung des Kreuzzugsgedankens*, Stuttgart 1936 (Forschungen zur Kirchen- und Geistesgeschichte 6)

EVANS, JOHN, 'The Arthurian Campaign', *Archaeologia Cantiana*, lxxviii, 1963, 83–95

FARAL, EDMOND, *La légende arthurienne: études et documents*, vol. i, *Les plus anciens textes* [Bibliothèque de l'Ecole des Hautes Etudes 255–7], Paris 1929 (reviewed by R. S. Loomis, with rejoinder and reply, *Modern Language Notes*, xlvi, 1931, 175–82)

FARAL, EDMOND, 'L'abbaye de Glastonbury et la légende du roi Arthur', *Revue historique*, clx, 1929, 1–49

FORSTER, MAX, 'War Nennius ein Ire?', *Festgabe Heinrich Finke*, Münster i.W. 1925, 36–42

FOSTER, IDRIS LLEWELLYN, '*Culhwch and Olwen* and *Rhonabwy's Dream*', in *Arthurian Literature in the Middle Ages*, ed. R. S. Loomis, Oxford 1959, 31–43

FOSTER IDRIS LLEWELLYN, 'The Emergence of Wales' in *Prehistoric and Early Wales*, ed. I. Ll. Foster and Glyn Daniel, London 1965, 213–35

GOUILLOND, ANDRÉ, ed., *Vie de Saint Germain d'Auxerre par le prêtre Constance de Lyon*, Lyon 1874

GRAEF, HILDA, *Mary: A History of Doctrine and Devotion*, London and New York 1963

GRISCOM, ACTON, *The Historia Regum Britanniae of Geoffrey of Monmouth*, London and New York, 1929

GRUFFYDD, W. J., 'The Mabinogion', *THSC*, 1912–13, 14–80

GRUFFYDD, W. J., *Math vab Mathonwy*, Cardiff 1928

GRUFFYDD, W. J., *Rhiannon*, Cardiff 1953

GUNN, W., *The Historia Brittonum commonly attributed to Nennius*, London 1819 [edition of the Vatican version]

GWYNN JONES, T., 'Some Arthurian Material in Keltic', *Aberystwyth Studies*, vi, 1924, 37–93

HAMEL, A. G. VAN, 'Arthur van Brittanië en Aneirin', *Neophilologus*, xxviii, 1943, 218–28

HAMEL, A. G. VAN, 'Aspects of Celtic Mythology', *Proceedings of the British Academy*, 1934, 207–48

HAMEL, A. G. VAN, 'Koning Arthurs Vader', *Neophilologus*, xii, 1927, 34–41

HAMEL, A. G. VAN, ed., *Lebor Bretnach: The Irish Version of the Historia Britonum ascribed to Nennius*, Dublin 1932

HANNING, ROBERT W., *The Vision of History in Early Britain: From Gildas to Geoffrey of Monmouth*, New York and London 1966

HAWKES, C. F. C., *The prehistoric foundations of Europe*, London 1940

HODGKIN, R. H., *A History of the Anglo-Saxons*, Oxford 1935

HUGHES, KATHLEEN, 'British Museum MS Cotton Vespasian A. xiv ("Vitae Sanctorum Wallensium")', *SEBC*, 183–200

HUGHES, KATHLEEN, 'The Distribution of Irish Scriptoria and Centres of Learning from 730–1111', *SEBC*, 243–72

JACKSON, KENNETH, 'Angles and Britons in Northumbria and Cumbria', *O'Donnell Lectures*, 60–84

JACKSON, KENNETH, 'Arthur's Battle of Breguion', *Antiquity*, xxiii, 1949, 48–9

JACKSON, KENNETH, 'The Britons in Southern Scotland', *Antiquity*, xxix, 1955, 77–89

JACKSON, KENNETH, 'Edinburgh and the Anglian Occupation of Lothian', *Dickins Studies*, 35–42

JACKSON, KENNETH, The Gododdin: *The Oldest Scottish Poem*, Edinburgh 1969

JACKSON, KENNETH, 'The Arthur of History' in *Arthurian Literature in the Middle Ages*, ed. R. S. Loomis, Oxford 1959, 1–11; 'Arthur in Early Welsh Verse', *ibid.*, 12–19

JACKSON, KENNETH, 'The "Gododdin" of Aneirin', *Antiquity*, xiii, 1939, 25–34

JACKSON, KENNETH, *Language and History in Early Britain*, Edinburgh 1953 (Edinburgh University Publications in Language and Literature 4)

JACKSON, KENNETH, *The International Popular Tale and Early Welsh Tradition*, Cardiff 1961

JACKSON, KENNETH, *The Oldest Irish Tradition: A Window on the Iron Age* (Rede Lecture 1964), Cambridge 1964

JACKSON, KENNETH, 'On the Northern British Section in Nennius', *Celt and Saxon*, 21–59

JACKSON, KENNETH, 'Once Again Arthur's Battles', *Modern Philology*, xliii, 1945, 44–57

JAMES, J. W., 'The Harleian MS Genealogy II', *BBCS*, xxiii, 1969, 143–52

JARMAN, A. O. H., 'The heroic ideal in early Welsh poetry', *Beiträge zur Indogermanistik und Keltologie Julius Pokorny zum 80 Geburtstag gewidmet*, ed. Wolfgang Meid, Innsbruck 1967, 193–211

JOHNSTONE, P. K., 'Vortigern and Aetius – a re-appraisal', *Antiquity*, xx, 1946, 16–20

JOHNSTONE, P. K., 'Mount Badon – a topographical clue', *Antiquity*, xx, 1946, 159–60 (see also Dobson, D. P., *Antiquity*, xxii, 1948, 43–5)

JOHNSTONE, P. K., 'Dual Personality of St Gildas', *Antiquity*, xx, 1946, 211–13

JOHNSTONE, P. K., 'The Date of Camlann', *Antiquity*, xxiv, 1950, 44

JOHNSTONE, P. K., 'The Victories of Arthur', *Notes and Queries*, clxvi, 1934, 381–2 (reply by H. Askew, *ibid*, 425–6; again by Johnstone, clxvii, 1935, 65)

JOHNSTONE, P. K., 'Mons Badonicus & Cerdic of Wessex', *Antiquity*, xiii, 1939, 92–6

JONES, FRANCIS, 'An Approach to Welsh Genealogy', *THSC*, 1948, 303–66

JONES, GWYN and JONES, THOMAS, *The Mabinogion*, London and New York 1949

JONES, THOMAS, 'The Black Book of Carmarthen, "Stanzas of the Graves"', *Proceedings of the British Academy*, liii, 1968, 97–139

JONES, THOMAS, 'The early evolution of the legend of Arthur', *Nottingham Medieval Studies*, viii, 3–21 (review of Welsh original by R. Bromwich, *Medium Aevum*, xxviii, 1959, 115–19)

KENDRICK, T. D., *British Antiquity*, London, 1950

KIRBY, D. P., 'Vortigern', *BBCS*, xxiii, 1968–69, 37–59

LA BORDERIE, ARTHUR DE, 'La date de la naissance de Gildas', *Revue Celtique*, vi, 1883–85, 1–13

LA BORDERIE, ARTHUR DE, *L'Historia Brittonum attribuée à Nennius et L'Historia Britannica avant Geoffroi de Monmouth*, London and Paris 1883

LEEDS, E. T., *Early Anglo-Saxon Art and Archaeology*, Oxford 1936

LIEBERMANN, F., 'Nennius the Author of the "Historia Brittonum" ', *Essays in Mediaeval History presented to T. F. Tout*, Manchester 1925, 25–44

LLOYD, SIR JOHN EDWARD, *A History of Wales*, London and New York 1939

LLOYD, SIR JOHN EDWARD, 'The Death of Arthur', *BBCS*, xii, 1944, 158–60

LOOMIS, C. GRANT, 'King Arthur and the Saints', *Speculum*, viii, 1933, 478–82

LOOMIS, R. S., 'Arthurian Tradition and Folklore', *Folklore*, lxix, 1958, 1–25

LOOMIS, R. S., 'Fundamental facts about Arthurian origins', *Studi in onore di Italo Siciliano*, ii, Florence 1956, 677–83 (Biblioteca dell'Archivum Romanicum, i, 86)

LOOMIS, R. S., 'Scotland and the Arthurian Legend', *Proceedings of the Society of Antiquaries of Scotland*, lxxxix, 1958, 1–21

LOOMIS, R. S., *Wales and the Arthurian Legend*, Cardiff 1956

LOOMIS, R. S., 'The Spoils of Annwn', *PMLA*, lvi, 1941, 884–936

LOT, FERDINAND, 'De la valeur historique du De Excidio et Conquestu Britanniae de Gildas', *Mediaeval Studies in Memory of Gertrude Schoepperle Loomis*, Paris and New York 1927, 229–64

LOT, FERDINAND, *Nennius et l'Historia Brittonum: Etude critique*, Paris 1934 [Bibliothèque de l'Ecole des Hautes Etudes 263]

LOT, FERDINAND, 'Nennius et Gildas', *Le Moyen Age*, viii, 1895, 177–84; ix, 1896, 1–13, 25–32

LOTH, J., 'Les deux Mano Irlandais et les deux Manau Brittons', *Revue celtique*, li, 1934, 185–95

LOTH, J., 'L'origine de la légende d'Arthur fils d'Uther Pendragon', *Revue celtique*, xlix, 1932, 132–49

LOTH, J., 'Remarques à l'Historia Brittonum dite de Nennius', *Revue celtique*, xlix, 1932, 150–65; li, 1934, 1–31

LUKMAN, N., 'The British General Gerontius (†410) in medieval epics', *Classica et Mediaevalia*, xii, 1951, 215–35

LUKMAN, N., 'British and Danish traditions: some contacts and relations', *Classica et Mediaevalia*, vi, 1944, 72–109

MACALISTER, R. A. S., *Corpus Inscriptionum Insularum Celticarum* I, II, Dublin 1945, 1949

MALMESBURY, WILLIAM OF, *Gesta Regum Anglorum*, London 1894

MALONE, KEMP, 'The Historicity of Arthur', *Journal of English and Germanic Philology*, xxiii, 1924, 463–91 (review by J. Loth, *Revue celtique*, xlii, 1925, 306–19)

MALONE, KEMP, 'Artorius', *Modern Philology*, xxii, 1925, 367–74

MEYER, KUNO, 'The Expulsion of the Dessi', *Y Cymmrodor*, xiv, 1901, 101–35

MICHEL, CHARLES, ed. and tr., 'Protévangile de Jacques', *Evangiles apocryphes*, i, Paris 1924, 1–51

MOMMSEN, THEODORE, *Chronica minora saec. IV. V. VI. VII*, Berlin 1894–8 [Monumenta Germaniae Historica Auctores Antiquissimi, x, xi, xiii]

MORRIS, JOHN, 'Dark Age Dates' *in Britain and Rome: Essays presented to Eric Birley* . . . ed. Michael G. Jarrett and Brian Dobson, Kendal 1966, 145–75

MORRIS-JONES, SIR JOHN, 'Taliesin', *Y Cymmrodor*, xxviii, 1918

MYRES, J. N. L., *Anglo-Saxon Pottery and the Settlement of England*, Oxford 1969

NASH-WILLIAMS, V. E., *The Early Christian Monuments of Wales*, Cardiff 1950

NEWELL, WILLIAM WELLS, 'Doubts concerning Nennius', *PMLA*, xx, 1905, 622–72

NITZE, W. A., 'Arthurian Problems', *BBSIA*, v, 1953, 69–75

NITZE, W. A., 'Bedier's Epic Theory and the Arthuriana of Nennius', *Modern Philology*, xxxix, 1941, 1–14

NITZE, W. A., 'Arthurian Names: Arthur', *PMLA*, lxiv, 1949, 585–96

NITZE, W. A., 'The Exhumation of King Arthur at Glastonbury', *Speculum*, ix, 1934, 355–61

NITZE, W. A., 'Geoffrey of Monmouth's King Arthur', *Speculum*, ii, 1927, 317–21

NITZE, W. A., 'More on the Arthuriana of Nennius', *Modern Language Notes*, lviii, 1943, 1–8

O'RAHILLY, THOMAS F., *Early Irish History and Mythology*, Dublin, 1946

PARRY, J. J., 'Geoffrey of Monmouth and the Paternity of Arthur', *Speculum*, xiii, 1938, 271–7

PARRY, J. J., 'The Vita Merlini', *University of Illinois Studies in Language and Literature*, x, 3, 1925, 251–380

PARRY, J. J., 'The historical Arthur', *Journal of English and Germanic Philology*, lviii, 1959, 365–79

PENDER, SEAMUS, 'Two unpublished versions of the Expulsion of the Déssi', in *Feilscribhinn Torna*, ed. S. Pender, Cork 1947, 209–17

PHILLIMORE, EGERTON, 'The *Annales Cambriae* and Old-Welsh Genealogies from Harleian MS 3859', *Y Cymmrodor*, ix, 1888, 141–83

PIGGOTT, STUART, 'The Sources of Geoffrey of Monmouth', *Antiquity*, xv, 1941, 269–86, 305–19

RALEGH RADFORD, C. A., 'Vortigern', *Antiquity*, xxxii, 1958, 19–24

REES, REV. RICE, *An Essay on the Welsh Saints*, London and Cardiff 1836

RHYS, SIR JOHN, *Celtic Folklore, Welsh and Manx*, Oxford 1901

RHYS, SIR JOHN (ed.), *Le Morte d'Arthur by Sir Thomas Malory*, London 1908

RHYS, SIR JOHN, *Studies in the Arthurian Legend*, Oxford 1891

RICHARDS, MELVILLE, 'Arthurian onomastics', *THSC*, 1969, 250–64

ROBERTS, RUTH, *Welsh place-names in the earliest Arthurian texts*, unpublished dissertation, Columbia University 1957

ROBERTS, RUTH, 'Twrch Trwyth, Tortain, Tors fils Ares', *BBSIA*, xiv, 1962, 91–7

ROSS, ALAN S. C., 'Hengist's Watchword', *English and German Studies*, ii, 1948–49, 81–101

ROSS, ANNE, *Pagan Celtic Britain: Studies in Iconography and Tradition*, London and New York 1967

RUSSELL, J. C., 'Arthur and the Romano-Celtic Frontier', *Modern Philology*, xlviii, 1951, 145–53

SECHELLES, D. DE, 'Les traditions légendaires bretonnes d'après "L'Historia Brittonum" ', *Annales de Bretagne*, lxiv, 1957, 145–62

SKENE, WILLIAM F., *The Four Ancient Books of Wales*, Edinburgh 1868

STENTON, SIR FRANK, 'The Historical Bearing of Place-Name Studies: England in the Sixth Century', *TRHS*, xxi, 1938, 1–21

STENTON, SIR FRANK, 'The English Occupation of Southern Britain', *TRHS*, xxii, 1940, 1–22

STEVENS, C. G., 'Ancient Writers on Britain', *Antiquity*, i, 1927, 189–96

STEVENS, C. E., 'Gildas Sapiens', *EHR*, lvi, 1941, 353–73

STOKES, WHITLEY, 'The Annals of Tigernach', *Revue celtique*, xvi, 1895, 374–419; xvii, 1896, 6–33, 119–263, 337–420

TATLOCK, J. S. P., 'Caradoc of Llancarfan', *Speculum*, xiii, 1938, 139–52

TATLOCK, J. S. P., *The Legendary History of Britain*, Berkeley and Los Angeles 1950

TATLOCK, J. S. P., 'The English Journey of the Laon Canons', *Speculum*, viii, 1933, 454–65

TATLOCK, J. S. P., 'The Dates of the Arthurian Saints' Legends', *Speculum*, xiv, 1939, 345–65

THURNEYSEN, R., 'Zum Geburtsjahr des Gildas', *ZCP*, xiv, 1923, 13–15 (reply by A. O. Anderson, *ZCP*, xvii, 1928, 403–6)

THURNEYSEN, R., 'Zu *Nemnius* (*Nennius*)', *ZCP*, xx, 1936, 97–137; 'Nochmals *Nemnius*', *ibid*, 182–91

TOLSTOY, NIKOLAI, 'Early British History and Chronology', *BBCS*, 1964, 237–310

TOLSTOY, NIKOLAI, 'Nennius Chapter Fifty-Six', *BBCS*, xix, 1960–62, 118–62

TRAUBE, LUDWIG, 'Zu Nennius', *Neues Archiv*, xxiv, 1899, 721–4

TREHARNE, R. F., *The Glastonbury Legends*, London 1967

WADE-EVANS, A. W., *Vita Sanctorum Britanniae et Genealogiae*, Cardiff 1944

WADE-EVANS, A. W., *The Emergence of England and Wales*, Cambridge 1959

WADE-EVANS, A. W., *Nennius's 'History of the Britons' together with 'The Annals of the Britons' and 'Court Pedigrees of Hywel the Good'; also 'The Story of the Loss of Britain'*, London 1936

WALSH, PAUL, 'The Annals attributed to Tigernach', *Irish Historical Studies*, ii, 1940, 154–9

WEISWEILER, HEINRICH, 'Das frühe Marienbild der Westkirche unter dem Einfluss des Dogmas von Chalcedon', *Scholastik*, xxviii, 1953, 321–60, 504–25

WHEELER, G. H., 'Gildas de Excidio Britanniae, Chapter 26', *EHR*, xli, 1926, 497–503

WILLIAMS, HUGH, ed., *Gildas: De Excidio Britanniae*, Cymmrodrion Society, London 1899

WILLIAMS, IFOR, *Lectures on Early Welsh Poetry*, Dublin 1944

WILLIAMS, IFOR, 'Mommsen and the Vatican Nennius', *BBCS*, ii, 1941–42, 43–8

WILLIAMS, IFOR, 'The Nennian Preface: a possible emendatïon', *BBCS*, ix, 1937–39, 342–4

WILLIAMS, IFOR, 'Notes on Nennius', *BBCS* vii, 1933-35, 380–88

WILLIAMS, IFOR, 'The Poems of Llywarch Hên', *Proceedings of the British Academy*, xviii, 1932, 269–302

WILLIAMS, IFOR, ed., *The Poems of Taliesin*, tr. J. E. Caerwyn Williams, Dublin 1968; Dublin Institute for Advanced Studies: Medieval and Modern Welsh series, iii

WILLIAMS, MARY, 'An Early Ritual Poem in Welsh', *Speculum*, xiii, 1938, 38–51

WRENN, CHARLES L., *Word and Symbol: Studies in English Language*, London 1967

ZIMMER, HEINRICH, *Nennius Vindicatus: über Entstehung, Geschichte und Quellen der* Historia Brittonum, Berlin 1893

ZIMMER, HEINRICH, 'Ein weiteres irisches Zeugnis für Nennius als Autor der *Historia Brittonum*', *Neues Archiv*, xix, 1893, 436–43

ZIMMER, HEINRICH, 'Ein weiteres Zeugnis für die nordwelsche Herkunft der Samuel-Beulan-Recension der *Historia Brittonum*', *Neues Archiv*, xix, 1893, 667–9

REFERENCES

Items marked with an asterisk indicate author's translation

2 *Arthur of Dalriada*

1 Jackson, *Gododdin*, 35
2 Williams, H., 81
3 Lot, *Nennius*, 201*
4 Chadwick, *Growth of Literature*, i, 32
5 But see, against Taliesin's link with Cynan Garwyn, Saunders
   Lewis, 'The Tradition of Taliesin', *THSC*, 1968, 298
6 Williams, H., *Llywarch Hên*, passim
7 Bromwich, *SEBH*, 122
8 Williams, Gwyn, *An Introduction to Welsh Poetry*, London 1953, 24
9 Anderson, *Adomnan*, 227, 229
10 O'Rahilly, 505
11 Stokes, 160
12 O'Rahilly, 383
13 Bromwich, *Triads*, 265n; Anderson, *Adomnan*, 227, suggests that
   Degsastan and the battle of the Miathi are identical, implying
   an even closer connection between Arthur of Dalriada and
   the British campaign against the Saxons
14 Williams, H., 401–3

3 *Arthur of Dyfed*

1 Pender, 211
2 Meyer, 101
3 Meyer, 113
4 Bartrum, *Genealogical Tracts*, 4
5 James, passim
6 Stokes, 178
7 *Paulys Realenzyclopädie*, ed. G. Wissowa, Stuttgart 1896, ii,
   1461–2
8 Kemp Malone, *Artorius*, passim

4 *The Unknown Leader*

1 Tacitus, *Annals of Imperial Rome*, tr. Michael Grant, London
   1959, 10
2 Williams, H., 9–11

3 Williams, H., 61–5
4 A. W. Wade Evans; however, towards the end of his life, even
   he admitted the unity of Gildas's work (*Archaeologia Cambrensis*, xcviii, 1945, 113–24)
5 Jackson, *Language and History*, 25
6 Chadwick, *SEBH*, 233ff
7 Williams, H., 72–3
8 Anderson, *ZCP*, 1928, 405–6

5 *The Bardic Image*

1 Bromwich, *SEBH*, 117
2 Bromwich, *Triads*, 35
3 Bartrum, *Genealogical Tracts*, 9
4 Suetonius, *The Twelve Caesars*, tr. Robert Graves, London 1957,
   171
5 Jones, F., *Genealogy*, 315–16
6 Quoted by Bartrum, *Genealogical Tracts*, 126
7 Bartrum, *Genealogical Tracts*, 85
8 Jones and Jones, *Mabinogion*, 153
9 The groups (in Bromwich, *Triads*) are:
      i. Later addition or substitution of Arthur: 2, 12, 50, 51, 52, 80
      ii. 'Arthur's court': 65, 73, 74, 77, 87, 88
      iii. Early material: 4, 26, 37R, 54, 56, 59 (and 53, 84 on
           Gwenhwyfar)
10 Translation by Dr Rachel Bromwich, p. 69 below
11 Jones, T., 'Early evolution', 17
12 All quoted from Bromwich, *Triads*
13 Bartrum, *Genealogical Tracts*, 87, 62
14 Williams, H., 409–11
15 Williams, M., passim
16 Jackson, 'Arthur in Early Welsh Verse', 13
17 Jones, T., 'Stanzas of the Graves', 127
18 Jones, T., 'Stanzas of the Graves', 108
19 Bromwich, *Triads*, 140
20 Translation kindly supplied by Dr Rachel Bromwich
21 Bromwich, *Triads*, 391
22 Jones, T., 'Stanzas of the Graves', 121
23 Bromwich, *Triads*, 391
24 Jones and Jones, *Mabinogion*, 135

25 Jackson, *Gododdin*, 76 ff
26 See A. O. H. Jarman, *Ymddidan Myrddin a Thaliesin* (Cardiff
   1967), 35–6, 60. I am indebted to Dr Rachel Bromwich for
   this and the previous reference.
27 e.g. Bromwich, *Triads*, 521
28 Loomis, 'The Spoils of Annwn', 889–91
29 Jones and Jones, *Mabinogion*, 130
30 Jones, T., 'Early evolution', 13
31 Lot, *Nennius*, 156–7*

6 *A Political Hero*

 1 Quoted by Chadwick, *SEBC*, 94, where the whole problem of
   the cultural life of Gwynedd is discussed
 2 Traube, Ludwig, ed., *Poetae Latini Carolini Aevi*, Berlin 1896,
   III, 342* [*Monumenta Germaniae Historica*]
 3 Forster, 37–40
 4 Lot, *Nennius*, 147*
 5 Lot, *Nennius*, 147*
 6 Lot, *Nennius*, 185*
 7 Ross, A. S. C., 83–91
 8 Liebermann, 39
 9 Bede, 553
10 See Bullock-Davies, *Professional Interpreters*
11 Zimmer, *Nennius Vindicatus*, 274
12 Chadwick, *SEBC*, 37
13 Mommsen (119) suggests that it came from the Convent of
   Montauban, but gives no grounds for this
14 Lot, *Nennius*, 121–3*
15 Lot, *Nennius*, 188–9*
16 Lot, *Nennius*, 147*
17 Zimmer, *Nennius Vindicatus*, 233*
18 Lot, *Nennius*, 161*
19 But see Sir Ifor Williams 'Hên Chwedlau', *THSC*, 1946, 28–58.
   I am indebted to Dr Rachel Bromwich for this reference
20 Lot, *Nennius*, 194–6*
21 Lot, *Nennius*, 183–4*
22 Collingwood, R. G. and Myres, J. N. L., *Roman Britain and the
   English Settlements*, Oxford 1937, 321ff
23 Bede, iii, 2
24 Dempf, passim

25 Graef, 161
26 Duchesne, 278
27 Graef, 42
28 Rees, 22–3, 63; see also Ifor Williams, *Armes Prydein & Llyfr Taliesin* (Cardiff 1955) (forthcoming English translation by R. Bromwich, Dublin Institute for Advanced Studies) ii, 25, 45
29 Jones, T., 'Early evolution', 5–6
30 Phillimore, 154
31 But see Alcock, *Arthur's Britain*, 50 for a different interpretation
32 Williams, H., 418
33 Jackson, 'Arthur's Battles', 57

7 *The National Messiah*

1 Lot, *Nennius*, 216*
2 Roberts, *Place-names*, 28
3 Jones and Jones, *Mabinogion*, 120
4 Roberts, *Place-names*, 72
5 Jones and Jones, *Mabinogion*, 132–5
6 William of Malmesbury, 127
7 Foster, '*Culhwch and Olwen*', 38–9
8 Jones and Jones, *Mabinogion*, 129
9 Bromwich, *Triads*, 45
10 Bromwich, *Triads*, 329–30
11 Above, pp. 32–3, 65

8 *Popular Beliefs*

1 Faral, 226*
2 Parry, 'Vita Merlini', 325–7*
3 Giraldus Cambrensis, *Opera*, ed. G. F. Warner, London 1891, viii, 126
4 Ralph of Coggeshall, *Chronicon Anglicanum*, ed. J. Stevenson, London 1875, 36
5 William Camden, *Britannia*, London 1610, 228
6 Hawkes, 366
7 *The Works of Sir Thomas Malory*, ed. Eugène Vinaver, Oxford 1967, 1242
8 Holmes, V. T., 'Old French: *Camelot*', *Romanic Review* 20, 1929, 231–6
9 Leland, John, *The Itinerary*, ed. L. Toulmin Smith, London 1907, 151

Index